The Fruits of Listening

Applying Qualitative Research Methods in the Design of
Contextually Responsive Theological Education

Colleen C. B. Weaver

WIPF & STOCK · Eugene, Oregon

THE FRUITS OF LISTENING
Applying Qualitative Research Methods in the Design of
Contextually Responsive Theological Education

Copyright © 2024 Colleen C. B. Weaver. All rights reserved. Except for brief quotations in critical publications or reviews, no part of this book may be reproduced in any manner without prior written permission from the publisher. Write: Permissions, Wipf and Stock Publishers, 199 W. 8th Ave., Suite 3, Eugene, OR 97401.

Wipf & Stock
An Imprint of Wipf and Stock Publishers
199 W. 8th Ave., Suite 3
Eugene, OR 97401

www.wipfandstock.com

PAPERBACK ISBN: 979-8-3852-2280-3
HARDCOVER ISBN: 979-8-3852-2281-0
EBOOK ISBN: 979-8-3852-2282-7

VERSION NUMBER 10/29/24

This book is dedicated to the memory of my father, Harold William Burgess, and to my mother, Marcia Kay Burgess. As educators, they taught me that it is not only what one teaches that matters, but how one teaches. Love is essential.

Contents

List of Tables | viii
List of Figures | ix
Preface | xi
Acknowledgments | xii
Abbreviations | xiii

1 Defining Theological Education and Contextualization | 1
2 The Legacy Inherited by Spanish Protestant Theological Education | 11
3 Spain's Protestant Community: An Historical Analysis | 33
4 The Faith Community's Perspectives on Theological Education | 51
5 Listening to Three Seminary Communities | 72
6 Harvesting the Fruits of Listening | 151
7 Conclusion: Planting Seeds | 169

Appendix 1: The Fruits of Listening—Five Contextualization Practices | 175
Appendix 2: Survey—Perspectives on Theological Education | 177
Appendix 3: Faculty Interview Questions | 186
Appendix 4: Student Interview Questions | 188
Bibliography | 191

Tables

Table 1: Faith Affiliation in Spain, 1993–2019 | 45

Table 2: Frequency of Attendance in Worship, 1993–2019 | 46

Table 3: Distribution of Non-Catholic Faiths in Spain, 1998–2018 | 47

Table 4: EVAF Data on Evangelical Believers in Spain, 1998–2019 | 48

Table 5: EVAF Data on Protestant Community of Madrid, 1993–2019 | 49

Table 6: Qualities and Skills Needed for Ministry Leadership | 55

Table 7: Formation to Be Facilitated by Theological Education | 57

Table 8: Abilities and Practices to Be Developed through Theological Education | 58

Table 9: Ranking of Most Important Courses Taught by Theological Educators | 59

Figures

Figure 1: Model of Four Continua—1 | 27
Figure 2: Model of Four Continua—2 | 31
Figure 3: Seminary A Continua | 105
Figure 4: Seminary B Continua | 129
Figure 5: Seminary C Continua | 148
Figure 6: Comparison of Three Seminary Continua | 150

Preface

I think that they somehow understood or sensed that I was genuinely interested, and so they spoke.

—Colleen Weaver[1]

Who is listening? Listening has become a precious and rare commodity in this world filled with voices. Listening takes time. If it is sincere, it is a process that cannot be rushed. Morton T. Kelsey writes, "When we truly listen to others, we are silent inside."[2] Yet, willingness to listen, to really listen, can produce fruits of discovery. The words of the people who spoke into this qualitative research through surveys and interviews became a sacred trust to me. They spoke not only because they had something they wanted to say, but because they trusted that I was committed to listen and to tend to their words until I could reap a harvest.

What is this book about? It is about listening and taking time to theologically reflect and ponder over the words, spoken or written, that are entrusted to us. The contextualization of theological education is the focus of this book, but the practice of listening can bear a variety of fruits in all areas of life. To contextualize theological education, listening, both to God and people, is critical and necessary as we strive to be holy, faithful, and responsive to the needs, questions, and desires of those whom we are committed to serve.

1. Colleen Weaver, coding reflections journal, May 9, 2019.
2. Kelsey, *Caring*, 73.

Acknowledgments

THIS BOOK PRESENTS THE fruits of my dissertation journey. I am thankful to my doctoral supervisors, Dr. Peter Rae and Dr. Julie Lunn, who offered their wisdom and expertise over many years. One Mission Society sent me to Spain in 1986 and that laid the foundation for my interest in and commitment to fruitful listening. I am thankful to the seminaries and individuals in Spain who participated in my research. This book tells brief portions of their courageous stories. Although the nature of research requires the application of a critical voice, I acknowledge my utmost respect for them and for their theological education visions and labors. I am also thankful for everyone who prayed and encouraged me to keep going. I am especially thankful for my husband Brent; my daughters Emily, Mary, and Katherine; my sons-in-law; and my grandchildren. They have lovingly walked with me in every step of the journey. Finally, I give thanks to Jesus Christ who called me to the vocation of theological education.

Abbreviations

AMyHCE	Anabautistas, Menonitas y Hermanos en Cristo España [Anabaptists, Mennonites and Brethren in Christ Spain]
ANECA	Agencia Nacional de Evaluación de la Calidad y Acreditación [National Agency of Quality Evaluation and Accreditation]
CeFoR	Center de Formation et de Rencontre Bienenberg [Francophone Bienenberg Training and Meeting Center]
CIS	Centro de Investigaciones Sociológicas [Center of Sociological Investigations]
ECTE	European Council of Theological Education
ECTS	European Credit Transfer System
ENQA	European Association for Quality Assurance in Higher Education
EQAR	European Quality Assurance Registrar for Higher Education
EVAF	Evangelismo al Fondo [Evangelism to the Depths]
FBSE	Formation Biblique Pour le Service Dans l'Eglise [Formation for Biblical Service in the Church]
FEREDE	Federación de Entidades Religiosas Evangélicas de España [Federation of Religious Evangelical Entities of Spain]
FTE	Full Time Equivalences

ABBREVIATIONS

IEE	Iglesia Evangélica de España [Evangelical Church of Spain]
INE	Instituto Nacional de Estadística
INQAAHE	International Network for Quality Assurance Agencies in Higher Education
ISCREB	El Instituto Superior de Ciencias Religiosas de Barcelona [The Institute of Religious Sciences of Barcelona]
OMS	One Mission Society
OTC	Open Theological College
SEUT	Seminario Evangélico Unido de Teología [United Evangelical Seminary of Theology]
SGIC	Sistema de Garantía Interna de Calidad [System of Internal Guarantee of Quality]
SWOT	Strengths, Weaknesses, Opportunities, and Threats
TEE	Theological Education by Extension
UEBE	Unión Evangélica Bautista de España [Baptist Evangelical Union of Spain]
VLE	Virtual Learning Environment

1

Defining Theological Education and Contextualization

> *Practical theology is particularly challenging and difficult work, for it takes the risk of listening to the critical concerns and practical realities of Christians living in particular contexts, and it must offer constructive theological proposals for living faithfully in that context.*
>
> —Kathleen A. Calahan[1]

Our world and the communities where we live and work experience suffering, shifting societal norms, financial inequities, migrating populations and the joys and sorrows of life's daily routines and relationships. Within this complex context, the church, locally represented by communities of Christ followers, bears witness to the teachings and love of Jesus Christ and to the peace-giving hope that Christ offers through his resurrected life. One of the ways that the church is equipped for the task of faithful witness bearing is through theological education.

Theological education has been practiced over centuries as the community of faith has sought to know and understand God, to train its leaders, to apply theological knowledge to daily faith practices, to transfer that knowledge to the local community, and to establish a theological heritage for future generations. The history of theological education documents its transitions as it has adapted to, reacted against, and, at times, ignored the contextual realities in which it has been functioning. Adjustments are

---

1. Calahan, "Three Approaches," 93.

also evidenced through shifts in focus on who is to receive theological formation, the primary purpose of that formation, the process for delivering formation, and where to locate formation in relation to the church and society. After centuries of variations, it is not surprising that there are differing conceptualizations and definitions of theological education. For that reason, it is important to begin with the definition of theological education that is foundational for this work. "Theological education" is the spiritual, doctrinal, and experiential formation of the community of faith so that they are equipped in the knowledge and love of Christ to carry out the work of the church in the world.[2] Among this community, some will be called to seek more specialized or scholarly ministerial theological education, such as pastors and theologians, and others who will serve through a diversity of ministries to build up the church.

To define and preserve its identity, theological education has also selected from a diversity of design options that shape and inform its organizational framework, mission, and institutional culture. It also implements formational practices, "practices" being the repeated communal activities and customs that are performed, consciously or unconsciously, that enact or represent a community's identity and beliefs. These formational practices are represented in its choice of educational methodologies; accessibility; means of engagement with students, the church, and society; and in its ordering of emphases between academics, devotion, and ministry practice.

"Contextualization" is the cultural adaptation process that takes place when designs, information, beliefs, or practices are brought from one distinct culturally situated community and introduced into another. Theological education's designs and practices have been developed in particular contexts, for particular faith communities, at particular times, and for particular purposes. With good intentions, these contextually particular designs and practices have been exported and imported and passed along over the years to new generations and across borders into different cultural realities. All too frequently this transference has occurred without performing the critical task of theologically reflective contextualization to facilitate transformative and relevant engagement with the receiving faith communities.

Failure to ask what Andrew Wingate calls "questions of contextuality" allows for the transference of unexamined aspects of a plan of study such as culturally situated beliefs or practices that might hinder

---

2. See Matt 28:19–20.

contextual adaptation and ignore cultural distinctives within the receiving community.³ An imported or exported design, curriculum, and its related practices, although doctrinally and educationally sound, may fail to engage students' minds, hearts, and hands if not first theologically and contextually adapted for the receiving community. However, as Bernhard Ott acknowledges, contextualization is not without risks; it requires an epistemological understanding of our own theological perspectives and beliefs to anchor us as we listen to others, delve into, and reflect on the implications of the contextual layers, and seek to practice theological faithfulness in all aspects of theological formation.⁴

Discovery of designs and practices of responsive contextualization utilized by theological education institutions to equip the church to thrive in its local community became the focus of this research journey, which utilizes the scholarship of theological educators, both practical and contextual theologians, as well as grounded theory and qualitative research methods to find answers to these questions: What are the distinctive components of contextually shaped designs and practices in theological education? How are these contextually shaped designs and practices developed and then implemented? When contextualization is either not happening or is limited in its scope and application, what factors hinder its development, and what are the implications of those limitations?

To narrow the focus of the investigation, the field research was conducted in the province of Madrid, Spain, where several Protestant evangelical seminaries offer theological education for Spanish and international students.⁵ All three of the theological education institutions presented in this research received their courses of study from sources outside of Spain. Qualitative research recognizes the researcher as one of the human participants in the investigation. My interest in this investigation has been and is

3. Wingate, "Overview," 239.
4. Ott, "Mission and Theological Education," 95.
5. The field research was conducted in 2017–18 prior to the global COVID pandemic. The terms "Protestant" and "evangelical" are used synonymously throughout this research to identify Christians who trace their faith heritage to the Reformation. Although the term evangelical is used in many contexts to denote a particular theological position and set of beliefs within wider Protestantism, the Spanish contextual use of the term as a generic name for Protestants is how the term is to be understood in this research. The term Protestant, in some Spanish contexts, can elicit negative associations with heresy rooted in Spain's historical inquisitorial oppression; for that reason, evangelical has typically been the preferred self-designation used by Spain's Protestants.

both professional and personal.[6] I spent fourteen years, intermittently from 1986 to 2017, working alongside Spanish theological educators and pastors. I have witnessed the challenges faced by Spain's Protestants, a minority community that has had limited consideration in scholarly research, as they have sought to establish their legitimacy, attain religious liberties, and increase their numerical presence in Spain.[7] Among the possible factors contributing to the persistent minority status of the evangelical community of Spain, I chose to focus on theological education and its contextualized relevance for the church. The lack of indigenous or local theologically trained leaders has at times meant that missionaries or other nonindigenous leaders have either remained in or stepped into various positions of ministry leadership, delaying the development and contextual impact of indigenous leadership. In some instances, available indigenous pastors were hastily placed into leadership roles and given preference because of their nationality without sufficient inquiries into their ministry backgrounds or theological formation. Expediency to fill ministry positions, at times, precipitated situations that wounded the faith community.[8] Contextualized theological education for Spain's Protestant evangelical community was and is critically necessary to provide the church with an adequate pool of theologically formed, spiritually mature, capable leaders who are indigenous or culturally astute if Spain is not their country of origin. Additionally, the increasing ethnic diversity of Spain's populations, both within and outside of the church, highlights the critical necessity of formation that can prepare students to navigate the increasing cultural complexities of the society.

A challenge to contextual understanding is posed by relational distance between the observed and the observer, whether its source is language,

---

6. I continue to serve in theological education, both in the academy as well as in the church. Since beginning the Spain-based research, I have relocated twice to countries with different languages, cultures, and distinctive church contexts. Practicing and applying the fruits of listening are critical in the contextualization of my teaching and ministry so that I can more effectively serve the church and offer theological formation that is contextually responsive and relevant.

7. The Roman Catholic and Eastern Orthodox Churches have long traditions of theological education out of which Protestantism was birthed. However, to keep the focus of this research on the context of Protestant evangelical theological education in Madrid, the research progressed closely, but not rigidly, within the boundaries of Protestant scholarship.

8. Even with thorough background checks and references, weaknesses can be missed; education, experience, and qualifications unfortunately do not guarantee exemption from possible moral failures and theological lapses.

culture, ethnicity, gender, age, or dissimilar life experiences. Stephen B. Bevans states that although cultural outsiders might offer misinterpretations due to their lack of insider understanding, they can sometimes be more perceptive about a culture than those who are immersed within it.[9] On the basis of previous immersion into the culture and language of Spain, this research presents what Bevans calls a "counterpoint" to the local perspectives.[10] Facilitating and enhancing theological learning is a cross-culturally shared aim. Participants in the survey and case studies contributed their unique contextual understandings and experiences. Their voluntary participation in this research motivated my commitment to discover contextually transformative designs and practices in theological education

Bevans also notes that a conflict, either external or internal, can prompt inquiry.[11] For me, that conflict or *inquietud* came from my identification with missionary movements that exported Protestant theological education to Spain.[12] I am not from Spain, and Spanish is a second language for me. As a missionary, I pragmatically transported the designs and practices of the theological education that I had received in my North American context to Spain. Through this research and its prioritization on the fruits of listening, I have been confronted by the previous poverty of my own theological reflection on Spain's history, culture, social structures, and diverse perspectives. I recognize in hindsight the missed benefits that the theological practices of cultural hermeneutics and intentional reflection on each unique context would have provided in the contextualization of my teaching and ministry in Spain. Returning to Spain to gather data for this research, I went to listen. Mary Clark Moschella writes that this type of ethnographic listening is "difficult because it requires us to give up the role of expert, and become a learner again."[13] I wanted to discover what the seminary faculty, students, and congregants were doing and saying or not doing and saying about the contextualization of theological education for the specific needs of Spain's Protestant evangelical church. I paid close attention to how and to what extent these institutions are reflecting

---

9. Bevans, *Models of Contextual Theology*, 19.

10. Bevans, *Models of Contextual Theology*, 20.

11. Bevans, *Models of Contextual Theology*, 20.

12. An *inquietud* is a concern, a sense or feeling of unsettledness. It literally means "unquietness."

13. Moschella, *Ethnography as a Pastoral Practice*, 142.

theologically and transformatively on their historical, ecclesial, and current societal contexts. In other words, I sought to harvest the fruits of listening.

Researching the contextualization practices of Spain's Protestant theological education fits within the scope of practical theology. Practical theology examines the practices and stories of a faith community as it attempts to simultaneously preserve, embody, interpret, and adapt its beliefs and actions to a society's changing context. Practical theologians serve the church through comprehensive, theological reflection on the church's lived theology. The scholarship of practical theologians shaped my theological thinking and methodological choices.[14] However, as this investigation progressed, it transitioned towards grounded theory and a mixed methods approach to probe the issues and complexities of theological education as it is perceived, practiced, and experienced in the Protestant community of Madrid.

Grounded theory methodology prioritized listening, observing, and reflecting with the aim of discovery. Conducting the research in the context of a particular community was critical for the validity of the results. By implementing the mixed methods of a survey that gathered quantitative and qualitative data from church attenders and of three case studies that included participant observation, interviews, and analysis of documents and institutional websites, the perspectives of three diverse groups—laity, seminary faculty, and seminary students—were heard.

It was also critical to research the historical context of Spain's Protestants and to locate the seminaries in the historical traditions of theological education. The present context could not be understood or analyzed without grounding it in a knowledge of their past experiences. Grounded theory methodology supported the fluidity of continuous reflection and analysis, working back and forth between data from the present and the past. The results, the fruits of listening, although situated in a specific location, community, and time, offer the potentiality of "transformative resonance" for other practitioners seeking to effectively contextualize theological education for their distinctive faith communities.[15]

Kevin J. Vanhoozer points out the critical, if not urgent, need for individual believers to develop a cultural hermeneutic, a process of biblical

---

14. Examples include: Graham et al., *Theological Reflection*; Cameron et al., *Talking About God*; Browning, *Fundamental Practical Theology*; Osmer, *Practical Theology*; Ward, *Introducing Practical Theology*; and Swinton and Mowat, *Practical Theology*.

15. Swinton and Mowat, *Practical Theology*, 45.

and theological discernment and interpretation, as they engage with and evaluate the constant stream of messages coming from the world around them.[16] This is a critical practice for theological education institutions as they provide prophetic guidance to the church and model for their students how they can fearlessly discern a faithful response to continually changing contexts. A theologically informed cultural hermeneutic can also be applied by an institution to evaluate the contextual appropriateness of its own design and practices for the faith community it serves.

Vanhoozer presents two foundational cultural message bearers that an institution, church, or individual would be wise to recognize because of their subtle shaping influence on attitudes and actions. The first is the "power interest" that lies behind or within the cultural messages communicated through a particular context. Who or what is seeking to influence the thinking and practices of the community, and what are the underlying motivations and aims?[17] The second is the "root metaphor that encourages [a particular group or society] to understand the whole world in terms of one part."[18] These metaphors wield power. Vanhoozer states: "When a metaphor takes hold, it changes the way we see things, and perhaps the way we live."[19] Stanley Hauerwas describes this practice of contextual discernment as a "habit of attentiveness"; it relies on one's "capacity for perception of particulars."[20] Hauerwas notes the inherent danger of these subtle yet influential messages in our practices and perceptions: "We inhabit narratives that often are ignored but in fact make all the difference for the position a person holds."[21] These "power interests" and "root metaphors" can be so deeply embedded in the customs and mindset of a society that their origins and messages remain unexamined, accepted as the status quo.[22] Awareness of the presence and power that these typically unstated messages wield may be particularly useful for seminaries as they assist the church in its navigation of cultural shifts and as the institutions examine their own designs and practices for indications that they too may have been influenced by cultural message bearers.

16. Vanhoozer, "Everyday Theology," 15–60.
17. Vanhoozer, "Everyday Theology," 50–51.
18. Vanhoozer, "Everyday Theology," 52.
19. Vanhoozer, "Everyday Theology," 52.
20. Hauerwas, *Work of Theology*, 15–16.
21. Hauerwas, *Work of Theology*, 14.
22. Vanhoozer, "Everyday Theology," 50–52.

In countries like Spain, historically embedded cultural messages may be national or they may be unique to a particular group, such as the Protestant community of Spain. Darrell Cosden and Donald Fairbairn observe that theological institutions often fail to recognize and examine the cultural and historical contextual influences that shape their theology and practice.[23] The aims and process of this work aligned with Cosden and Fairbairn's definition of contextual theology: "a theology which self-consciously recognizes, examines, and critiques the historical and cultural factors which have influenced the expression of Christian life among a given group of people."[24] Contextual theology requires engagement with people. Its practitioners listen and observe the concrete particulars of situations and communal practices. They dialogue with people to discern how best to communicate Christian doctrine and practice so that the church can faithfully follow Christ within the local culture and community.[25] Sigurd Bergmann and Mika Vähkängas note that the discussion of contextual theology is often limited to missiological reflection on cross-cultural engagement.[26] Although Spain's Protestant evangelical seminaries are, in part, a product of missiological efforts, indigenous Spaniards now give leadership to the theological education institutions in this study.[27] Many of the contextual issues that they face come from within their own local community. Contextual theology and practical theology are disciplines that can assist the church, wherever it is located, to communicate its messages with greater clarity.

Bevans proposes six models of contextual theology. Each model represents a distinct approach in the communication of exported and imported messages and practices to a receiving community.[28]

1. In the translation model, "supracultural" and "supracontextual" qualities are attributed to the gospel message, with the implication that the only adjustment needed is for the message to be translated

---

23. Cosden and Fairbairn, "Contextual Theological Education," 125.
24. Cosden and Fairbairn, "Contextual Theological Education," 126–27.
25. Bevans, *Models of Contextual Theology*, 18.
26. Bergmann and Vähkängas, "Doing Situated Theology," 3.

27. I am using the term *indigenous* with reference to Spaniards to refer to those for whom Spain is, generationally, their country of origin. The term *nonindigenous* refers to those whose country of origin is one other than Spain.

28. Bevans, *Models of Contextual Theology*, 31.

DEFINING THEOLOGICAL EDUCATION AND CONTEXTUALIZATION

into a vernacular language in order to be accessible to all generations and nations.[29]

2. The anthropological model prioritizes indigenous knowledge and cultural understanding; messages and practices must pass through this local filter in order to be successfully transmitted and received.[30]

3. The praxis model responds to the deficiencies and injustices within a community and adapts the message to address those problems with the goal of producing transformative social and personal changes.[31]

4. The synthetic model gathers all the "voices" from the past and present and then develops a message based on those findings that makes theological sense. It values both what is unique to a particular culture as well as what it shares with others.[32]

5. The transcendental model focuses on the collective inner thoughts and feelings of a receiving community. Even though those who practice this model acknowledge cultural distinctiveness among people, they hold that all people, everywhere and throughout history, think essentially in the same ways.[33]

6. Finally, the countercultural model assumes that the message, when delivered, has prophetic power to produce a crisis of critical self-awareness in the receiving community as it views itself in the light of the gospel message.[34]

Bevans's models provide a series of theological approaches to contextualization that serve as a point of reference in the analysis of the practices implemented by the seminaries in the case studies. It is important to note, however, that this research was not constrained by the framework of Bevans's models. Instead, it proceeded utilizing the methodology of grounded theory to permit the results to emerge from the data before any comparisons with Bevans's models were made.

The following chapters explore four contexts that have and continue to shape Protestant theological education in Spain, and particularly in the

---

29. Bevans, *Models of Contextual Theology*, 43.
30. Bevans, *Models of Contextual Theology*, 55–56.
31. Bevans, *Models of Contextual Theology*, 70.
32. Bevans, *Models of Contextual Theology*, 90.
33. Bevans, *Models of Contextual Theology*, 104–5.
34. Bevans, *Models of Contextual Theology*, 120–21.

three seminaries featured in the case studies. Chapter 2 is a brief overview of the history of theological education. This context is the historical heritage of the three seminaries, the origins of their current designs and practices. A framework of continua is introduced to visualize shifts along four primary foci over the centuries that have influenced the development of theological education's designs and practices: who to teach, for what purpose, how to teach, and where to locate theological education in relation to the church and society. Chapter 3 focuses on the national historic and cultural context of Spain's Protestant community from the Reformation through the first two decades of the twenty-first century. This is the context in which these Protestant evangelical seminaries and the churches they serve were formed and where they continue to function. Chapter 4 explores the third context, the local, ecclesial context of the three seminaries, through the analysis of quantitative and qualitative survey data collected from people who attend Protestant evangelical churches in the province of Madrid. The survey participants contributed their perspectives and experiences with theological education. Chapter 5 features the three institutional case studies; this is the fourth and actual context of each institution, including its faculty and students. Chapter 6 presents the fruits of listening, the research discoveries based on all the triangulated data. Finally, chapter 7 summarizes the salient results and their implications for the contextualization of the designs and practices of theological education. Questions for reflection are provided at the conclusion of each chapter to assist readers in applying the findings of the research to their own contexts.

2

The Legacy Inherited by Spanish Protestant Theological Education

> *[A practice] is ancient, and larger than you are; it weaves you together with other people in doing things none of us could do alone. But each practice is also ever new, taking fresh form each day as it subtly adapts to find expression in every neighborhood and land.*
>
> —Craig Dykstra and Dorothy C. Bass[1]

THE FORMATIONAL PRACTICE OF remembering holds potential for refreshing, reorienting, and revealing the varied components that speak into and shape our present understandings and actions. This is the root system, unseen, yet vitally connected to the fruits that are produced. Exploring the history of theological education, an ancient practice of the church, is a purposeful exercise in remembering. The vantage point of reflection for many theological institutions is often their present context. Institutional aims may also direct reflection towards the future, yet there is value in a 360-degree reflection that includes a purposeful examination of the past. First, our reflection begins with the practice of critical remembering. It is a purposeful approach to historical reflection. Second, an overview of the history of Christian theological education is presented. It has been divided into five periods, extending Sidney Rooy's original framework of four distinctive historic models of theological education up to the present.[2] The

---

1. Dykstra and Bass, "Times of Yearning," 7.
2. Rooy, "Historical Models," 51–77.

Spanish Protestant seminaries that participated in the case studies have inherited this history, and it informs and guides design aspects of their curricula, organizational structures, instructional aims, and formational practices. It is their legacy. Finally, a framework of four continua is introduced that can be utilized in the analysis of current theological institutions and in the identification of their historical affiliations.

The Practice of Critical Remembering

The phrase "critical remembering" refers to the intentional, analytical, and reflective review of the past. Critical remembering is a process of sifting through memories and historical events to identify how the past has shaped present perceptions and practices. Two sources inspired the use of this phrase. First, in the Scriptures, God's people are repeatedly called to the practice of remembering. The past is recalled to reorient one's theological thinking and to examine the appropriateness of one's current actions or beliefs in light of what is reviewed.[3] Theological education is situated in this tradition of faithful and formational critical remembering. Second, the disciplines of practical theology and grounded-theory qualitative research encourage investigation into the underlying origins of current practices and perceptions. Theological critical remembering can apply a lens of faithfulness to the process of institutional discernment.

The phrase "critical remembering" has been used by scholars working in contexts where there have been past political, social, or cultural injustices, as experienced by Spain's Protestants. Mary Beth Tierny-Tello uses the phrase in her discussion of the role of critical memory: "Critical remembering . . . brings the more emotionally determined memory [of childhood] into contact with critically acquired [mature] knowledge."[4] This can facilitate the reinterpretation of injustices and inequities, and a new understanding can be empowering and informative.[5] Phillipe Tortell, Margot Young, and Mark Turin discuss several ways that critical remembering appropriates the past to bring about accountability for errors, preservation of heritage, and rediscovery of what has been lost or forgotten. They write, "Memory must inform our present for us to imagine a better future."[6] Melina Porto

---

3. For example, see Deut 8 or 1 Cor 11:24–25.
4. Tierny-Tello, "Remembering Childhood," 5.
5. Tierny-Tello, "Remembering Childhood," 10.
6. Tortell et al., "Remembering Is Crucial," para. 15.

and Leticia Yulita conducted research on the response of language students when they were introduced to past atrocities as part of their historical and cultural introduction to a new language: "The students explicitly highlighted the importance of remembering the past . . . and also acknowledged the transformational role of memories in the reconstruction of a better future."[7] That is the process and aim of critical remembering.

Edward Farley stresses the need for this type of historical review and analysis as one of the components of the contextualization of theological education:

> All . . . [theological institutions] are caught in the backwash of historical forces which have modified and maybe removed the original rationale for their patterns of theological study. . . . I am persuaded that reform attempts will continue to be merely cosmetic until they address the fundamental structure and pattern of studies inherited from the past and submit to criticism the presuppositions which undergird the pattern.[8]

The implications of Farley's observations take on an additional degree of complexity when theological education is exported or imported from one context to another. The three theological institutions featured in this research are situated in the greater historical narrative of Christianity and in the distinctive narrative of Protestant evangelical theological education. The seminaries' legacies include more than lists of suggested courses and ministerial skills to be developed. Educational philosophies, epistemologies, theologies, worldviews, doctrinal distinctives, and various communal practices are embedded in the designs and practices passed along to Spain's Protestant seminaries. If theological education institutions neglect the practice of critical remembering, they may unknowingly perpetuate contextually situated theological understandings and practices that inhibit their ability to flourish within their own distinctive contexts.

Shifting Priorities in the History of Theological Education

Theological Education's Heritage in Biblical Narratives

There is no established date or initiating event to mark the origin of theological education. J. E. Roscoe begins his history with the Old Testament

---

7. Porto and Yulita, "Place for Forgiveness," 491.
8. Farley, *Theologia*, x–xi.

example of Samuel and the school of prophets about which there are few details.⁹ Robert Banks argues that accounts of priestly, prophetic, and religious formation recorded in the Old and New Testaments are foundational examples of theological education.¹⁰ Likewise, Farley highlights the Hebrew practice of "ordered learning" that took place in homes and synagogues and argues for its inclusion in Christianity's educational heritage.¹¹ Linda Cannell emphasizes the influence of Hebrew epistemology in the early church's practices of formation, a relational knowledge of God expressed through righteous living within the community.¹² Ott agrees that the biblical accounts offer models of educational wisdom and practice, yet he cautions against labelling those accounts as theological education because of the contextual and temporal gap between the past and the present.¹³ Nonetheless, this educational heritage informed the practices of the first generation of Christians.

Theological Education in the Early Church

Rooy's framework for the history of theological education serves as the foundational model for this review. From the early church of the first century to the twentieth century, he identifies four periods, each defined by a salient characteristic of its design: catechism, monasteries, scholasticism, and the seminary.

In the first period, Rooy highlights the methodology of the catechism that was used to instruct and form believers during the early centuries of the church.¹⁴ Harold H. Rowdon situates the time frame for this period in "the four centuries or so when the Church existed within the Ancient Roman World [AD 32–500]."¹⁵ The dates given are general place markers, rather than strict demarcations. In this initial catechetical context, theological formation took place informally in homes as believers studied and lived their faith within their local communities. Describing this period Randy L. Maddox writes, "Its concern was essentially practical;

---

9. Roscoe, *Short History*, 9.
10. Banks, *Reenvisioning Theological Education*, 73–82.
11. Farley, *Fragility of Knowledge*, 86.
12. Cannell, *Theological Education Matters*, 64–69.
13. Ott, *Developing Theological Education*, 139.
14. Rooy, "Historical Models," 54–56.
15. Rowdon, "Historical Perspective," 75.

i.e. oriented to understanding and norming Christian life in the world."[16] Banks argues for the faithfulness of this relational model to the educational practices used by Jesus in the formation of his disciples. Based on this model of formation for and within the faith community, Banks has proposed a contemporary design for theological education, the Jerusalem or missional model,[17] that prioritizes the practice of *"in"* ministry formation that takes place within the context of the local church and community.[18] Justo L. González briefly references this period of informal and nonformal theological education in his mention of Timothy's formation under the tutelage of his grandmother and mother.[19]

The changing social context of the early church as it expanded numerically, geographically, and ethnically across the Roman world presented the church with formational challenges as it sought to educate and enculturate both Jews and gentiles into one Christian community. They had to develop a practice of formation that would be consistent across Christianity. The solution was the catechesis, organized instruction in doctrine and practice to prepare believers for participation in the life and sacraments of the Christian community.[20] Eventually this mode of instruction was further formalized with the establishment of catechetical schools where Christian faith was explored and contextually adapted through the use of Greek forms of thought and argumentation.[21]

González repeatedly states that the ability to read was generally the primary qualification for ministry leadership positions. Those who had received education in the Greek or Roman system could read and explain the Scriptures and catechetical writings to the majority illiterate population.[22] Although González does not discuss the role of orality in the early church's theological formation, Rooy cites evidence from Justin Martyr, Origen, and Eusebius that faith was orally transmitted.[23] Rowdon also comments on the significant role of relational nonformal instruction even within the catechetical schools:

16. Maddox, "John Wesley," 123.
17. Banks, *Reenvisioning Theological Education*, 70.
18. Banks, *Reenvisioning Theological Education*, 70, 132 (emphasis original).
19. González, *History of Theological Education*, 1.
20. Rooy, "Historical Models," 54–55.
21. González, *History of Theological Education*, 5–6.
22. González, *History of Theological Edu*cation, 2.
23. Rooy, "Historical Models," 54.

> The breadth of its syllabus must not lead us to suppose that the Catechetical School was an impersonal, coldly academic institution. It revolved around the person of the Master (who was appointed by the Bishop) in whose house it met, and who provided the lion's share of the instruction. In the case of Origen, at least, it is clear that the force of his Christian character, the strength of his devotion to Christ, and the rigors of his personal standards of behavior formed an important part of the training.[24]

The locus of Christianity gradually shifted geographically and culturally away from its original Jewish context. The educational and moral Greek philosophy of *paideia*, holistic formation through education of the mind and body to facilitate virtuous action and spiritual understanding, was adapted by Christian scholars and incorporated into the teaching and formational aims of the then predominantly gentile church.[25] Banks labels this the Athens or classical model.[26] Learning in this design tends to occur more individually and internally, as opposed to the communal formation of the early church. The influence of Greek *paideia* has continued to shape designs and practices over the centuries.

The catechetical model, first implemented to instruct believers in their new life in Christ, underwent contextualization as it became increasingly immersed in Greek and Roman communities. Although cultural adaptation is a necessary aspect of contextualization, it can require compromises and forfeitures even as it facilitates culturally appropriate engagement and new theological understandings. Theological education had begun informally within the context of the entire faith community. However, as the necessity for the apologetic formulation of doctrine became increasingly more critical, the target student group was narrowed to equip a select group with specialized formation to articulate, defend, and preserve the faith.

Theological Education in a Newly Christianized Europe

The second period of theological education, from approximately AD 500 to 1000, begins in the tumultuous final years of the Roman Empire.[27] This period began when the threat level to civilization and stability was high as

24. Rowdon, "Historical Perspective," 76.
25. Kelsey, *Between Athens and Berlin*, 6.
26. Banks, *Reenvisioning Theological Education*, 19.
27. Rowdon, "Historical Perspective," 77.

Visigoth and Germanic tribes spread from north to south across Europe. Rooy names this period the monastic model because monasteries became centers for theological study.[28] The monasteries' isolation was critical to their role in the preservation of religious texts.[29] Study and formation were reserved for literate men who lived in the monasteries. Village priests often came into their positions through apprenticeships or other types of appointment, often with little or no prior formal education.[30] Augustine and Benedict, among others, recognized the critical need to prioritize theological education for clergy and scholars, however, that education came power and status.[31] Cannell explores the dynamics of the biblical education that was offered to an educated elite and its secondary effect, the strengthening of the clerical hierarchy.[32] In contrast to the clerical formation, Rooy states that during this period "lay participation in theological education practically disappeared for more than a thousand years."[33] Communal education was not absent—but neither was it prioritized.

With the eventual establishment of Christianity as the predominant faith in Europe, the sense of urgency and need for catechetical formation sharply declined. The educational requirements for baptism and church membership were simplified to facilitate acceptance for most of the population, including men, women, and children.[34] One resource that attempted to bring correction and educational nurture to the faith community was Gregory the Great's *Pastoral Rule*.[35] Where available, it became a standard manual for clerical education. Gregory's teachings encouraged priests to model virtuous lives and to provide pastoral care for the parishioners.

The installation of town cathedral schools towards the end of this period increased the physical proximity of theological education to the general population, but González notes that access to study itself was reserved for literate clergy and civil servants.[36] David S. Dockery observes that this

---

28. Rooy, "Historical Models," 56–58.
29. González, *History of Theological Education*, 30.
30. Rooy, "Historical Models," 58.
31. Rooy, "Historical Models," 57.
32. Cannell, *Theological Education Matters*, 131.
33. Rooy, "Historical Models," 57.
34. Rooy, "Historical Models," 58.
35. González, *History of Theological Education*, 26.
36. González, *History of Theological Education*, 32–33.

was a foundational period in the establishment of an ecclesial hierarchy.[37] Ecclesial and political power held among a small group of elites had become the goal. However, Roscoe makes a serious assertion about the formational poverty of the clergy: "The majority of the clergy who came in contact with the people, [sic] possessed no other qualifications for their office than a certain skill in performing ceremonies of the church."[38] These weaknesses came to the attention of Charlemagne who had both political power and papal blessing. He gave Alcuin the task of establishing schools and norms for the clergy and of ensuring the preservation of the biblical texts.[39] Marvin Oxenham writes, "As a result of Alcuin's reforms, the European continent became dotted with centers of structured study in monasteries and in cathedral schools."[40] The stage was set for the next major educational transition. In previous centuries persecution and heresy had intensified the need to educate the faith community. Peace and the wide acceptance of Christianity created two new threats: complacency towards the importance of educating the wider faith community and, as a consequence of the first threat, the loss of knowledge among the greater population.

Theological Education during a Scholastic Revival

Rowdon brackets this period from AD 1000 to 1500, the later Middle Ages.[41] Rooy characterizes theological education during these years as the scholastic model.[42] Research, intellectual freedom, and new structures for schooling flourished after the crusaders returned with a rich trove of classic scholarship, such as Aristotle's writings, formerly lost to or unknown in Europe.[43] Aquinas entered into this context of renewed Aristotelian scholarship and reintroduced *theoria*, "discursive reasoning," and *scientia* to theological education.[44] Aquinas became a catalyst for educational

---

37. Dockery, "Theological Education," 7.
38. Roscoe, *Short History*, 25.
39. González, *History of Theological Education*, 34.
40. Oxenham, *Liquid Modernity*, 122.
41. Rowdon, "Historical Perspective," 78.
42. Rooy, "Historical Models," 59–62.
43. Cannell, *Theological Education Matters*, 133.
44. Kelsey, *To Understand God Truly*, 39–40.

transformation.[45] Oxenham describes the process for these educational developments:

> As time passed, reputable *magistri* gained fame, and, with increasing frequency, students began to flock to them in order to engage in systematic study. As these groups became established in European cities, they organized themselves in guild-like fashion to obtain recognition and rights from the local authorities. . . . This marks the birth of the university.[46]

Theological education was given the highest position within the university system. Years of prior scholarship and proven ability as a lecturer and debater were prerequisites for earning a culminating theological degree.[47] Key educational characteristics of this period were an educated elite, transmission of information, and an aim of intellectual prowess with learning located primarily in the academy. Dockery notes that ministerial education in pastoral care that would facilitate the spiritual formation of the community was not the university's aim.[48] Although Oxenham notes the value of the consolidated curriculum and reading lists among the universities, Rooy offers a critical summation, characterizing theological education as increasingly esoteric, abstract, and unrelated to daily life.[49] Spiritual nurture and catechetical formation of the community of faith were again deprioritized.

During the fourteenth and fifteenth centuries, the disparity between the scholasticism of the universities and the educational poverty of the parish continued. A significant redress for that poverty was the intentional use of religious imagery and ritualistic participation in sacred services and festivals, a catechetical variation. Through liturgical and artistic mediums, such as stained-glass windows, rituals, icons, and allegory, people learned the stories of the Scriptures and the saints and experienced the mystery of the divine. Yet, as Rooy notes, little was done to develop the laity's spiritual comprehension or to facilitate their application of Christian teachings in their daily lives.[50]

---

45. Oxenham, *Liquid Modernity*, 97.
46. Oxenham, *Liquid Modernity*, 122.
47. Roscoe, *Short History*, 31.
48. Dockery, "Theological Education," 8.
49. Rooy, "Historical Models," 59–60.
50. Rooy, "Historical Models," 61.

Providentially, balancing voices have been lifted throughout the history of theological education. Rowdon notes that the formation of religious orders of friars attempted to provide pastoral clergy education and instruction to the lay community.[51] Kelsey highlights Duns Scotus who encouraged clergy to practice their faith in all of life's daily activities based on Scotus' theology of God as the "doable knowable."[52] Clergy were encouraged to interact with the local community and to model the life of faith for all. The Brethren and Sisters of the Common Life initiated by Groote in the Netherlands brought theological education to the common people by teaching them to read, providing resources in the vernacular languages, forming communities that encouraged service to others, and faithfulness to the study of the Scriptures. They earned the respect of religious and political leaders who allowed them to extend their teachings to other areas of Europe.[53]

Change was on the horizon. Erasmus had begun to promote education for all ages through the production of written materials. The invention of the printing press facilitated access to educational materials for the masses.[54] From elitist university lecture halls to local communities that received vernacular copies of Scripture, dramatic shifts in the designs and practices of theological formation continued to occur.

Theological Education from the Reformation into the Twentieth Century

The Reformation initiated the period of theological education that Rooy names the seminary model based on Ignatius Loyola's design and practices of intentional theological formation.[55] This period began in the 1500s and extends beyond the 1900s due to the enduring utilization of the seminary model's structured form of theological education for clergy. As a corrective to past formational deficiencies in the theological education of church leaders, the Reformation inspired the establishment of prescribed standards and accountability for clergy.[56] In contrast to the isolation of

---

51. Rowdon, "Historical Perspective," 80.
52. Kelsey, *To Understand God Truly*, 45.
53. Cannell, *Theological Education Matters*, 236–39.
54. González, *History of Theological Education*, 66–68.
55. Rooy, "Historical Models," 62–63.
56. González, *History of Theological Education*, 73–74.

monasteries, the seminary model did not necessarily call clergy away from the local community.[57] The practice of equipping the priesthood of all believers was renewed through the work of Luther, Melanchthon, and others who prioritized the study of the Bible in theological formation for both clergy and laity of all ages.[58]

This period began with a flurry of biblical and theological research as both Protestant and Roman Catholic scholars delivered apologetic arguments to refute one another's doctrinal positions.[59] Theological education, as it had in the universities, continued to progress on a track that affirmed the primacy of cognitive knowledge. Although there were expanded educational opportunities for laity, ecclesial power structures tended to be held by limited numbers of educated people. Walter C. Jackson illustrates the imbalance of power in his reference to the Reformed community in Geneva:

> According to John Calvin, theologians alone knew the "Truth" of God. . . . Theological education, then, consisted in learning obedience to the teachings of the great theologians among whom John Calvin was the chief "Master." . . . Ministry, of course, was to see to it that the faithful in the churches obeyed the dogmas and creeds of God's appointed "Masters."[60]

Brian Edgar has classified this design of theological education as the Geneva or confessional model because of its prioritization on the knowledge of God, doctrinal fidelity, and ecclesial traditions.[61] However, in response to centuries of theological education that had generally emphasized cognitive knowledge and ecclesial superiority, the pendulum did begin to swing back in some faith communities, particularly among Pietists. They cultivated knowledge through relational love with Christ and with others and situated instruction within the context of the local church.[62]

From the Reformation to the Enlightenment changes came rapidly. The Enlightenment scholars built upon the epistemological transitions initiated by Aquinas. They set the foundation for the next century's embrace of *wissenschaft*: critical methodical investigation to test all theories to

57. Rooy, "Historical Models," 64–65.
58. Rooy, "Historical Models," 64.
59. González, *History of Theological Education*, 69–74.
60. Jackson, "Brief History of Theological Education," 509.
61. Edgar, "Theology of Theological Education," 212–13.
62. Kelsey, *To Understand God Truly*, 42.

determine what is verifiably true.[63] Theology was losing its position as the "queen of the sciences." It had to defend its right to remain in the university context of intellectual freedom and critical inquiry.[64]

Schleiermacher rose to the challenge of this new transformative threat to theological education. He proposed three disciplines of theological study: *"practical theology"*—the skills and knowledge needed by ministers; *"historical theology"*—the study of Christianity; and *"philosophical theology"*—the interpretation and expansion of the implications and projections of historical theology.[65] The practice of dissecting the whole into its parts for the purposes of analysis was a characteristic of post-enlightenment thinking. However, Schleiermacher's application of this practice to theological education unintentionally evolved into the compartmentalization of theological studies into four distinct disciplines: biblical studies, theology and doctrine, church history, and practical theology. Farley names this organizational framework "the four-fold pattern."[66] Focus began to shift away from an emphasis on the interrelatedness of these disciplines to a specialization in one of the four.[67] The fourfold design was frequently transported by European and North American missionaries to other regions of the world. Banks calls this the Berlin or vocational model of theological education.[68] It prioritizes academic theological education and professional ministerial training for clergy in contrast to the internal personal spiritual formation of the Athens model. In this seminary model, theological education gradually transitioned out of the universities to dedicated confessional seminaries.

In the nineteenth century, a renewed emphasis on missions in Europe, Britain, and the United States created an urgency to equip laity for missionary service. The Bible school opened an alternative pathway to theological education for people with varying levels of academic proficiency in contrast to the academic and professional requirements of the universities.[69] Bible schools traditionally focused on personal spiritual

---

63. Kelsey, *Between Athens and Berlin*, 13–14.

64. Kelsey, *To Understand God Truly*, 80–81.

65. Farley, *Theologia*, 91–93. Farley's discussion of Friedrich Schleiermacher is based on Schleiermacher's *Brief Outline on the Study of Theology*.

66. Farley, *Theologia*, 23.

67. Ott, *Beyond Fragmentation*, 39.

68. Banks, *Reenvisioning Theological Education*, 34.

69. Ott, *Beyond Fragmentation*, 48.

formation, *paideia*, and practical preparation of laity for mission.[70] Spiritual nurture in a dedicated, often insulated, environment was and continues to be one of the core features of a Bible school's design, classified by Graham Cheesman as a variant of the monastic model.[71]

Theological Education from the Twentieth Century to the Present

Based on the diversity of the designs and practices of theological education from the last half of the twentieth century to the present, my proposed label for this period is the eclectic model of theological education. The term "eclectic" represents not only the variety of available options but the combinations of designs that are practiced—for example, a residential seminary that offers remote learning. Pragmatism, available resources, competition for students, developments in educational philosophy and learning theory, and global connectivity are some of the factors contributing to this model characterized by diversity.

By the twentieth century, universities, seminaries, and Bible schools were common designs for theological education in Europe and North America. Missionaries transported these designs and their related practices around the globe and sent some local believers to Europe or North America for training with the expectation that they would return to their indigenous context with both a theological education and a design for a theological institution that could be transplanted in their local contexts. Sunday schools, correspondence courses, and other communal faith gatherings, such as camp meetings, offered nonformal and informal theological formation to the church, increasing the variety of options in this eclectic model.

A new design for theological education emerged in 1962 as the result of a pastoral leadership crisis in Guatemala. The Protestant evangelical faith community was experiencing rapid growth. The classic institutional residential seminary model, patterned after the Berlin or Geneva designs, was too costly. Its admissions requirements and course of study were too rigid to quickly and effectively train the number of leaders needed to serve so many. In response to the need, Theological Education by Extension (TEE) was designed by the Presbyterian Seminary of Guatemala. After a series of trials and errors, programed study booklets were designed to accommodate varying levels of academic abilities so that students could remain at home in their

70. Ott, *Beyond Fragmentation*, 49.
71. Cheesman, "Competing Paradigms," 60–61.

local jobs while they progressed independently through the course materials.[72] A professor would travel to accessible locations to offer periodic seminars to reinforce learning, encourage progress, and provide fellowship. David McCulloch offers a definition: "TEE is decentralized theological education. It is a field-based approach and does not interrupt the learner's ongoing relationships and commitments and thus cultural dislocation is minimized."[73] TEE's characteristics of transportability, flexibility, and primarily self-directed instruction in the student's local context led to global implementation of the model. However, J. Norberto Saracco comments that the content of the curriculum, borrowed from traditional seminaries, exhibited few adaptations to address contextual issues specific to the local churches.[74] McCulloch critiques TEE's tendency towards paternalism in its failure to empower people in humble circumstances to envision or enact transformative change within their faith community and local society.[75]

In recent decades, technological advances have transformed educational methodologies and communication. Theological education has moved online in both synchronous and asynchronous classrooms. Simulcasts have facilitated the creation of global classrooms for seminaries and churches. Megachurches have produced curriculum and training materials that have been widely dispersed to form a network of national and international learning communities. Oxenham reviews postmodernism's impact on our epistemologies and practices and the reasons why we struggle to find solid ground in this context, which he describes as "liquid education."[76]

Yet, at the core of theological education's present and past shifting priorities is its relationship with the church. It is a critical yet at times tenuous partnership. According to Alistair McGrath, theological education has often failed to serve the church and its people by turning inward upon itself, sometimes anecdotally characterized as being an ivory tower.[77] Roscoe's concluding statement in his history of theological education, written in 1948, challenges contemporary practitioners to evaluate the contextual responsiveness of their own institutions to the needs of the church and

---

72. McCulloch, "Oslo Model," 58.
73. McCulloch, "Oslo Model," 57.
74. Saracco, "Nuevos modelos," 30.
75. McCulloch, "Oslo Model," 102.
76. Oxenham, *Liquid Modernity*, 39. See his discussion on the characteristics and implications of liquid education, *Liquid Modernity*, 118–40.
77. McGrath, "Theological Education," 4.

society: "[Theological institutions] would sooner see their influence waning and dying out and becoming extinct rather than encourage the spirit of adventure in new needed fields."[78] Whatever theologies, philosophies, and methodologies facilitate and shape institutional transformations, shifts in the design and practices of theological education are critical to ensure that the formation being offered remains relevant and addresses the questions that the church and society are asking. Rupen Das writes, "Since the time of the Early Church to the present, theological education has always considered: 1) the needs of the Church in a particular context, as well as 2) the influence of the local culture."[79] In light of the details and shifting emphases in the history of theological education, Das's statement suggests an ideal that has not always been consistently applied in the contextualization of theological education. There were periods when adjustments were only made for particular minorities, such as the clerical elite. Societal responsiveness and consequent changes have not always been for the good, as this historical review suggests—for example, in the normalizing of Christianity and consequent loss of consistent and serious formational practice applied in the theological education of the entire faith community. Critical remembering and analysis of past events and their impact serve to inform and check our responses to new challenges and contextual realities.

Although there are always new challenges to consider, three global trends, noted repeatedly by theological educators, present critical and immediate opportunities for theological education to contextualize its designs and practices.[80] First, there is a recognized need for informal, practice-based, nondegree training offered through a variety of formats and venues within the context of the local church. This calls for a shift or broadening of theological education's aim to include all the church. Second, biblical illiteracy and hostility towards Christianity are increasing, although it is important to note that neither represents a historically new challenge to theological education. Third, migration and the formation of multicultural communities present opportunities for institutions to become skilled in cultural literacy and intercultural communication in order to engage in and offer transformative theological education to diverse populations. Each year brings additional

78. Roscoe, *Short History*, 63.

79. Das, "Relevance and Faithfulness," 19.

80. Aleshire, "Future Has Arrived," 69–80; Escobar, "Educación Teológica," 19–36; González, *History of Theological Education*, 138-39; Le Cornu, "Shape of Things to Come," 13–26; Morgan, "Through a Glass Darkly," 255–65; Ott, *Developing Theological Education*, 62–65, 84–86.

challenges and opportunities that call theological education to examine the faithfulness and relevance of its work as it empowers and theologically equips people for the work of the church in the world.

The task ahead is monumental, but it is not unlike the experience of the first century, as theological formation transitioned from its original Jewish context to the plurality of the known world at that time. Unlike them, today we have the advantage of knowing and learning from their successes and failures.

Four Continua Representing Core Priorities of Theological Education

The history of theological education reveals the following shifts: who the targeted students were, the educational methodologies that were implemented, the aims or outcomes that were desired, and the locations that were chosen for instruction. These shifts occur along four continua that represent core formational priorities represented by the following questions: Who is to be educated? How are they to be educated? For what purpose are they to be educated? And what is the best location for that education? These four priorities and their variations reflect the historic tensions in theological education as it has and continues to navigate its relationship with the church and society.

David Goodbourn proposed the implementation of continua as a tool for analyzing the design and practices of adult Christian education in the local church.[81] He recognized that continua offer flexibility, provide a common means of communication for each theme in an analysis, and reduce semantic misunderstandings because they do not rely on specific terminology. In short, they are flexible. The continua function as sliding scales and always hold the entire range of possibilities between their two poles. They avoid the limitations of a strict either-or model. I adapted Goodbourn's original three continua and have introduced a fourth continuum to represent a facet of theological education not represented in his original framework. The utilization of these four continua guided the process of critical remembering as I reflected on paradigm shifts in the history of theological education.

---

81. Goodbourn, "Mapping," 39–47.

Figure 1 Model of Four Continua

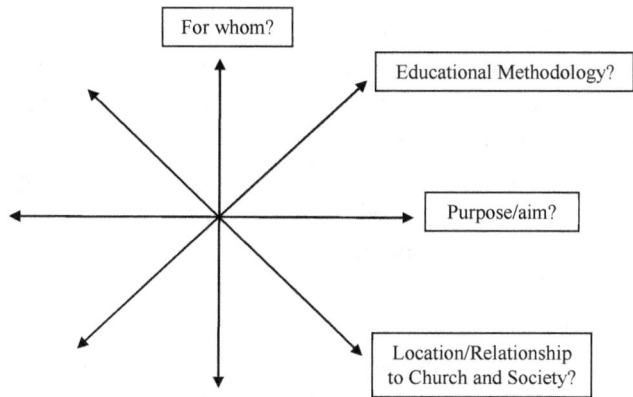

For whom is theological education designed? Goodbourn labeled this the "client group" continuum for church education. He placed the "whole society" on one extreme and participating church members on the other.[82] To adapt the "client group" for theological education, I have placed *a select minority*, often referred to as clergy or professional leaders, at the extreme end of one pole and *all the church*, often referred to as laity, at the opposite end.[83] Although they are not specifically named in this model, the people of the greater society are represented in *all the church*. They are the population in which the church community resides and to whom the church community ministers through word and deed.

Scholars vary in their answers to theological education's question, For whom? Ott defines theological education as education specifically for those who are training for pastoral ministry and Christian leadership.[84] Orlando E. Costas broadens the formational target to three specific groups of leaders: laity who are called to a teaching ministry within the church, pastors and church leaders who equip the church, and scholars and theologians.[85] In contrast, Craig Dykstra argues for the intentional inclusion

---

82. Goodbourn, "Mapping," 41.

83. In the context of ecclesial adult Christian education, Goodbourn names the church and society as the respective ends of this first continuum. Goodbourn, "Mapping," 41–43.

84. Ott, *Developing Theological Education*, 7.

85. Costas, "Theological Education and Mission," 9–12.

of all Christians.[86] Farley, likewise, asserts that all believers benefit from an informed theological understanding that can guide their daily living, an understanding that pastors and Christian workers have a responsibility to teach and model for their parishioners.[87] The history of theological education reflects these positions along the "for whom" continuum, from the early church's communal formation to the elitist groups of theological scholars in the universities.

Which educational methodology is utilized in the design? This continuum, labeled "the educational approach" by Goodbourn, ranges in his model between an emphasis on experiential methods at one end and intellectual, cognitive methods on the other.[88] Generally, it represents the pedagogical and learning style dichotomies between heart and head and to some extent between doing and knowing. Within the history of theological education, some of the shifts along this continuum have been represented by variations in the prioritization of either theory or practice, *paideia* or *wissenschaft*, and a focus on either individual or communal formation. Instructional methods varied over the centuries—for example, catechisms, iconography, pastoral manuals, scholarly university lecturers, and asynchronous online learning.

What is the aim or purpose of theological education? When Goodbourn applied this question to a church's adult Christian education, he categorized the continuum's polarities under the heading of "content" and placed faith development at one end of the spectrum and human development at the other.[89] In the context of theological education, which includes the formation of clergy, I replaced the polarity of human development with ministry development to represent specialized formation for ministry leaders, although this would not be exclusively limited to clergy. I retained faith development at the opposite pole, with the understanding that the aim of this polarity is the holistic development of an individual or community. In practice, theological education generally seeks to fulfil a full range of aims represented on this continuum to equip people spiritually, intellectually, and practically for a life of service and to provide wisdom and guidance for the church and society.

---

86. Dykstra, "Reconceiving Practice," 53.
87. Farley, *Theologia*, 175–77.
88. Goodbourn, "Mapping," 43–45.
89. Goodbourn, "Mapping," 41, 45–46.

There are essentially two schools of thought regarding theological education's primary purpose. The first group would argue that the aim is to produce transformation within students. Costas identifies three critical purposes: that it would "form" the character, that it would "inform" the mind, and that it would then have the power and influence to bring about "transform[ative]" results individually and corporately within the church as well as in the surrounding community.[90] In the history of theological education, this polarity aligns with *paideia* and the design of the Athens model. The second group would assert that the aim is to form a community of scholars who can discern, evaluate, and interpret the trajectories and messages of the society and the church. H. Richard Niebuhr, in collaboration with Daniel Day Williams and James M. Gustafson, envisions theological institutions as intellectual centers that think and reflect on behalf of the church.[91] This reflection, according to Enrique Fernández, provides the church with guidance for relevant engagement with local and global communities.[92] Wonsuk Ma sees the practice of societal discernment as particularly critical in the preparation of the next generation of Christians.[93] Joseph C. Hough and John B. Cobb emphasize the role of theological education in the preservation of the historical memory of the church in order "to lead the church to become more of what this memory now calls it to be."[94] Endowing ministry leaders with the keeping and transference of the church's memory was prioritized in periods when the church had to defend or clarify its doctrine, as it did during the period of the early church and in the beginning of the Reformation.

Where does the seminary locate itself in relation to the church and to the society? I have created a fourth continuum to represent theological education's location in relation to the church and to the society. This placement is typically represented by its actual physical location, but this continuum also represents an institution's degree of relational engagement with the church or the society. The institution may function within a church, in the same area or town, or in a remote physical location, as in the monastic model, where it was essentially self-contained. Institutions now also have the option of functioning in virtual campuses.

90. Costas, "Theological Education and Mission," 8.
91. Niebuhr, *Purpose of the Church*, 116.
92. Fernández, "Engaging Contextual Realities," 341.
93. Ma, "Role of Theological Education," 16:14–48.
94. Hough and Cobb, *Christian Identity*, 18.

Examples of relational placement can be observed in the types of communication and degree of interdependence among the church, society, and the academy. Kelsey suggests three scenarios for the relationship between the seminary and church: (1) The institution identifies itself as a church. (2) The institution provides training but expects churches to care for the spiritual needs of students. (3) The institution is a safe harbor for students until they go back out into the world.[95] Monasteries and Bible schools have tended to locate in remote locations. House churches and online learning have potential for more direct relational proximity. Universities and seminaries typically have their own buildings or properties often within reasonable physical proximity to the church, yet they are also separate entities. The choice of location impacts the design, the practices, and the relationship with both church and society.

When the four continua are brought together, they offer a multifaceted overview of how they separately and together impact the design and practices of theological education in a particular institution or in a particular period, like the monastic model. The following diagram represents the interconnection of these four continua. Circumstances, aims, personnel, or context may necessitate that some institutions position themselves at various points along any of the four continua. Additional continua could be included if needed, for example, accredited–nonaccredited or denominational–interdenominational. The determination of a point's location on a particular continuum is directly related to the specific context of a given institution. The solid black circles on the following diagram are illustrative for the purpose of demonstration. This hypothetical institution prioritizes education for the church and, to a lesser degree, its leaders (select minority). It implements experiential methods, emphasizes faith development, and is external yet closely connected to the church.

---

95. Kelsey, *To Understand God Truly*, 51–57.

Figure 2 Model of Four Continua—2

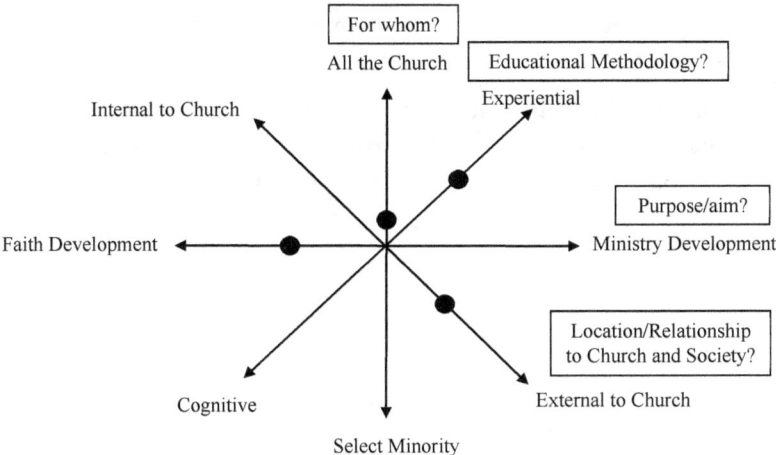

The practice of critical remembering prefaced the review of the history of theological education from the early church to the present. The history was concluded with an introduction to four continua that provide a framework for the analysis of theological education's shifts in who to educate, how to educate, the aim of education, and where to educate. Within the history of theological education, answers to these questions were influenced by power structures, epistemologies, resources, social and environmental circumstances, and the relationship between the church, society, and theological institutions. Present and future theological education is rooted in this history of shifts and variations. The research was conducted in the Protestant evangelical community located in the province of Madrid, Spain. This is their history, but it is shared by all who seek to theologically educate and equip the church for faithful service and witness in the world.

Questions for Reflection

1. With which model would your theological institution or church have the greatest affinity: catechetical, monastic, scholastic, seminary, or eclectic? Name one or two ways that model is contextually suited to your current situation or one or two ways that model may need to be adjusted.

THE FRUITS OF LISTENING

2. Where would your institution be on each of the continuums? How would you describe your place markers on each continuum: nonnegotiable, continuously shifting, of perhaps in need of adjustment? Give a reason for each of your descriptions.

3. What would be the ideal next chapter in the history of theological education: a new model, a return to its origins, or something else? Give one or two reasons for your statement.

3
Spain's Protestant Community: An Historical Analysis

> *Contextualization points to the fact that theology needs to interact and dialogue not only with traditional cultural value, but with social change, new ethnic identities, and the conflicts that are present as the contemporary phenomenon of globalization encounters the various peoples of the world.*
>
> —STEPHEN B. BEVANS[1]

ALTHOUGH CATHOLICISM HAS BEEN the dominant religion in Spain for centuries, historically, the country has been home to three faiths: Christianity (represented by Catholicism and Protestantism), Islam, and Judaism. While each religious community's historical experience merits study and reflection, this research focuses on Spain's Protestant community and its historical and cultural context. Historian Helen Graham writes, "Doing history is, by definition, an unending dialogue between the present and the past."[2] Through surveys and case study interviews, Madrid's Protestant evangelical community spoke about their current experiences with theological education. This historical review fills in elements of their background story. This was a necessary step, to explore through critical remembering themes and related questions that had emerged after the initial analysis of the survey and interview data: How does prolonged

---

1. Bevans, *Models of Contextual Theology*, 27.
2. Graham, *Spanish Civil War*, 149.

persecution and minority status effect future generations? What is the significance of recurring references to scarcity and fragility? Why was it necessary for almost all faculty to defend their institution's legitimacy when they had not been asked to do so? What lies behind the repeated descriptions of the church as defensive and weak in its theological formation? Spain may be in Europe, but knowing its past is critical to understanding the present context of its Protestant evangelical community.

A Brief History of Protestantism in Spain

Protestantism during the Spanish Inquisition

Northern Europe has been a center for Protestantism since the beginning of the Reformation in 1517. However, the history of Protestantism in Spain has been marked by persecution and developmental disruptions. The Spanish Inquisition was, in many ways, an extended attempt to maintain the purity of the country's Catholicism. For over three hundred years, 1478–1834, those who represented doctrines or philosophies deemed contrary to the Catholic Church were prosecuted and sentenced with fines, imprisonment, or death, with Jews and Muslims being the first faith communities to be scrutinized.[3]

When the Reformation began to infiltrate Spain, Protestantism was quickly marked for expurgation. Spanish kings Charles V and his son Philip II led the efforts to eradicate all "Lutherans," the label, as noted by Robert C. Spach, erroneously applied to all Protestants.[4] Philip recalled all Spaniards studying overseas to prevent their indoctrination into foreign ideas. Borders were closed to trade. Bibles and other banned literature were seized.[5] As a consequence of these decisive steps, Spain was virtually but not completely untouched by the Reformation. Francis Luttikhuizen writes, "What had begun at the turn of the sixteenth century as an initial step towards religious reform . . . had turned into a nightmare."[6]

Some Protestant sympathizers lost their lives; others fled the country. Although the dissemination of their beliefs was severely restricted, Spanish Protestant scholars living outside of Spain managed to produce

3. Luttikhuizen, *Underground Protestantism*, 26–27.
4. Spach, "Juan Gil," 868.
5. Luttikhuizen, *Underground Protestantism*, 93–94.
6. Luttikhuizen, *Underground Protestantism*, 103.

the Reina-Valera, a well-respected vernacular Spanish version of the Bible that is now a significant legacy of that period.[7] It was not surprising that, when British missionary George Barrow came to Spain in the late nineteenth century, he found that Spaniards had little or no familiarity with the Bible.[8] Even now, centuries later, older generations tell stories of how they were discouraged as children from reading the Bible. The Inquisition was extremely effective; its impact lingers on. Antonio González Fernández writes, "Everything in that time became truncated trajectories, and the [Inquisition's] bonfires imposed an end to whatever seed of evangelical theological reflection [had been sown] in these lands."[9]

Mauricio Drelichman, Jordi Vidal-Robert, and Hans Joachim Voth analyze the enduring impact of living through over three hundred years of perpetual inquisitorial tribunals on Spanish society. Through comparative statistical analysis they found that communities that had experienced high levels of inquisitorial activity had lower levels of income, education, and trust in contrast to those who had not had the same experiences.[10] By trust, they mean the ability of people to work together and communicate openly with one another.[11] They write, "Our data imply that a total of 36 million Spaniards today live in areas affected historically by the Inquisition; only 8.1 million live in areas that have no recorded impact."[12] Madrid, where this research was conducted, is one of the documented areas where there were pockets of high to moderate inquisitorial impact. Drelichman et al. state, "Nobody expects the Spanish Inquisition to still matter today, but it does."[13]

A Brief Period of Religious Freedom

In the late 1860s a new constitution initiated a period of religious freedom, referred to by Protestants as the "second Reformation."[14] It opened the door for missionaries from Europe and North America to reintroduce

---

7. Vincent, "Ungodly Subjects," 108.

8. Luttikhuizen, *Underground Protestantism*, 296–97.

9. All translations from Spanish to English are by the author unless otherwise noted. Fernández, "Desafío," 66.

10. Drelichman et al., "Long-Run Effects," 1.

11. Drelichman et al., "Long-Run Effects," 5.

12. Drelichman, et al., "Long-Run Effects," 3.

13. Drelichman, et al., "Long-Run Effects," 1.

14. Estruch, "Protestants in Spain," 53.

Protestantism to Spain.[15] Jason Ferenzi describes the theological education exported by that wave of missionaries as being "deeply embedded in the cultural and academic structures" of the contexts of those who exported it.[16] He cites Africa, Asia, and Latin America as the continents that received the nineteenth-century-Protestant doctrinal and institutional exports. Spain, although part of the European continent, should be included in the list of regions impacted by that theological exportation. In contrast to northern Europe, Spain had missed centuries of Protestant development due to the Inquisition. Two of the seminaries in this research were founded during this time of religious freedom. Antonio González reflects on the contextual insensitivity of those well-intentioned missionaries:

> When the small and brief spaces of political openness made possible some religious liberty, Protestant theology and spirituality arrived already "associated" or "attached," not to the Spanish context, but rather to the contexts of Europe and North America where Protestantism had sent out deep roots. . . . Evangelical theology spoke now about strange problems, in a certain way imported from other contexts. It responded to questions that were not asked and affirmed faithfulness to principles that no one initiated, to condemn itself to an existence in a certain way marginal and foreign. . . . One thinks that a new theology or a new spirituality can bring the desired contextual relevance. However, time and again, what one proposes responds to other contexts.[17]

Within a few decades, another period of persecution would test the resilience of the fledgling Protestant community. The brief period of religious tolerance did little to alter the dominance of the Catholic Church in Spain. In his analysis of Spanish literature written between 1875 and 1931, John Macklin notes the recurring positive thematic association of Catholicism with genuine Spanishness set against recurring negativity towards "the Reformation, the Enlightenment, the French Revolution, Protestants, Freemasons, foreign ideas, [and] liberalism."[18] Duncan Wheeler describes the underlying, uncomfortable dichotomy of that period: "The prototype of two Spains—one traditionalist, conservative and inward-looking; the other progressive and modern, its eyes firmly set on

---

15. Vincent, "Ungodly Subjects," 108.
16. Ferenczi, *Serving Communities*, 33.
17. Fernandez, "Desafío," 437–38.
18. Macklin, "Religion and Modernity," 186.

Europe—was firmly entrenched by the nineteenth century."[19] Spain was sharply divided politically, religiously, economically, and philosophically. These tensions brought the country to a climatic breaking point after Spanish liberals formed the Republic in 1931. The leaders of the Republic made a critical error in their antagonistic anticlerical position towards the Catholic Church.[20] Lay people interpreted this threat to Catholicism as an attack on their way of life.[21] Franco and other military leaders united in their commitment to Catholic religious fidelity and nationalistic fervor. Together, they initiated a civil war to preserve and protect the integrity of traditional Spain.[22] It was a violent and complicated conflict.

Protestantism During the Francoist Era

By 1939, Franco had established an authoritarian government in Spain at the cost of six hundred thousand Spanish lives.[23] The Spanish Inquisition provided a model of government for Franco's National Catholicism under his leadership from 1939 to 1976. The Catholic Church actively participated in Franco's repressive regime, reporting those suspected of anti-Spanish actions or loyalties.[24] Thousands were killed or imprisoned; indigenous languages, other than Castilian Spanish, were prohibited; and government censorship monitored media, education, and the overall society.[25]

Mary Vincent chronicles Protestant marginalization and oppression from 1939 to 1953. She writes, "[Protestantism's] association with 'England' led to its depiction as an external current of 'propaganda,' both dangerous and, at the same time, doomed to failure."[26] Protestants suffered limitations of their rights, stereotyping, false accusations, violence to their properties and persons, and even martyrdoms. In addition to

---

19. "Liberalism" in this research refers to a progressive, left-leaning form of government and philosophy. "Conservatism" in this research refers to a more traditional form of government that, within the context of Spain, would be authoritarian and religiously traditional and conservative. Wheeler, *Following Franco*, 26.

20. Payne, *Collapse of the Spanish Republic*, 11, 16–17.

21. Graham, *Spanish Civil War*, 12.

22. Graham, *Spanish Civil War*, 3.

23. Casanova, *Spanish Republic*, 332.

24. Graham, *Spanish Civil War*, 134.

25. Faber, *Exhuming Franco*, 29.

26. Vincent, "Ungodly Subjects," 115.

their persecuted status, they were generally economically poor and uneducated, suffering what Vincent labels as "double marginality."[27] These two characteristics are noteworthy considering the findings of Drelichman et al. on the lingering impact of Inquisitorial oppression.

Within their own context, however, Spanish Protestants exhibited characteristics that mirrored the authoritarianism and rigidity of the dictatorship under which they suffered. The conservatism of their doctrines and practices ironically aligned with National Catholicism's strict moral standards. In his article "How Can There Be Protestants in Spain?," Juan Estruch quotes Rev. Alberto Araujo, a pastoral leader in one of the denominations exported to Spain in the nineteenth century:

> In our Churches, too, it is easy to find the dogmatism, the fanaticism, and the intolerance of which we accuse others. . . . The Protestant Church in Spain is not adequate intellectually. Spanish Protestantism is suffering from illiteracy, a biblical illiteracy in the first place, including ecumenical illiteracy. . . . One of our Spanish characteristics is an inferiority complex which we try to hide. Deep down we fear that our faith might not resist the shock. We tend too much to seek security in dogma, which is a childish form of security: an ostrich-security.[28]

In the 1950s, Protestants organized the Commission for Evangelical Defense to advocate on behalf of Protestants. J. D. Hughy describes the commission's work to procure justice and freedom for Protestants:

> Led by a Baptist pastor, José Cardona, [it] defended Protestants arrested or harassed for religious reasons, appealed for the opening of churches, petitioned the authorities repeatedly for greater religious liberty, and cultivated relationships with influential friends of freedom.[29]

Spanish Protestants had to defend their authentic Spanishness. Estruch, writing in 1968, describes the struggle for legitimacy:

> The idea is above all to demonstrate that a good Protestant can also be a good Spaniard. This is a normal reaction in face of the current prejudice which maintains that it is incompatible to be a Protestant and a Spanish citizen at the same time. This is a constant

---

27. Vincent, "Ungodly Subjects," 113.
28. Estruch, "Protestants in Spain," 56.
29. Hughey, "Church, State, and Religious Liberty," 489.

preoccupation, often unconscious, which incessantly recurs in most writings by Spanish Protestants.[30]

Even in the twenty-first century, Spanish Protestant believers face similar questions about their legitimacy. In a 2018 interview, *El Diario* reporter Angel Villascusca interviewed Protestant pastor Emmanuel Buch who reflected on the years of oppression when the national police would stand outside the doors of the Protestant church to deter people from entering. Buch blames that marginalization of Protestant evangelicals on the fact that even today many people in Spain still know little about evangelicals.[31] Antonio González writes, "It is significant that, in Spain, the crass religious ignorance of the media has been given to calling evangelicals [Protestant Christians] 'evangelists.'"[32] During the Inquisition, all Protestants were erroneously labeled "Lutherans."[33] Years of oppression have left their mark on Spain.

Protestantism and Spain's Democracy

Spain's transition from a dictatorship to democracy is regarded as exemplary due to the peacefulness of the process and the generally successful incorporation of a range of political factions into a new government. Spaniards voted to establish a constitutional monarchy in 1978.[34] To achieve this peaceful transition, a general amnesty was established to cover crimes and injustices that had occurred in the war. Wheeler writes, "All sides of the political divide [had to] make an effort not to instrumentalize the past in the present."[35] The nation was told to forgive and forget rather than seek justice.[36]

A brief coup in 1981 failed to hinder Spain's path to democracy and its eventual membership in the European community. The federalization process pacified concerns through the distribution of certain powers of self-determination to seventeen Autonomous Communities of Spain.

---

30. Estruch, "Protestants in Spain," 56.
31. Villascusa, "Nuevo auge," para. 10–11.
32. Fernandez, "Desafío," 447.
33. Spach, "Juan Gil," 868.
34. Wheeler, *Following Franco*, 15–16.
35. Wheeler, *Following Franco*, 29.
36. Seoane, "Spain during the Transition," 369.

Susana Sueiro Seoane writes that these "collective identities . . . had been negated and repressed under the Franco regime."[37] Spain swung from authoritarianism to liberalism when the socialists gained majority control of Spain's elected government in the 1980s. The country continued to face challenges, suffering bloody acts of politically targeted assassinations during the years of Basque separatist activity. Yet progress continued. In 1986, Spain entered the European Union, and in 1992 they hosted both the summer Olympics and the World Expo.

During these national adjustments, freedoms slowly began to be restored to Protestants and other religious minorities. Exploring the theory of religious "heritage discourses," Avi Astor, Marian Burchardt, and Mar Griera analyze the processes and powers that shaped Spain's transition to a politically and religiously pluralist democracy. As a result of the 1980 Organic Law on Religious Freedom, Protestants and other minority religious communities, such as Judaism and Islam, were given the opportunity to receive state recognition if they could give proof they were historically "deeply rooted" in Spain.[38] "The granting of rights to religious minority communities was framed as being an act of historical restorative justice" for years, if not centuries, of religious persecution.[39] Spanish Protestant evangelicals established their historic presence and began to pursue full legal recognition and its accompanying liberties.

Building on the precedent of the 1950s Commission for Evangelical Defense, evangelical lawyers and church leaders formed La Federación de Entidades Religiosas Evangélicas de España (FEREDE), in 1986.[40] FEREDE advocates for Protestant evangelical entities in governmental and civic matters.[41] The majority of Spanish evangelical churches and organizations register with and are represented by FEREDE, although membership is not required by Spanish law.[42]

Although the 1980s Organic Law on Religious Freedom set Spain on a course towards significant religious pluralism and liberty, it was as late as 1992—when King Juan Carlos ratified an agreement on behalf of the

---

37. Seoane, "Spain during the Transition," 371.
38. Astor et al., "Politics of Religious Heritage," 132.
39. Astor et al., "Politics of Religious Heritage," 133.
40. FEREDE's website is https://www.ferede.es.
41. FEREDE, *Vademécum Evangélico*, 267–68.
42. FEREDE, *Vademécum Evangélico*, 271.

state with FEREDE—that significant rights were conceded to evangelicals.[43] In this agreement, FEREDE argued for the legal rights of evangelical clergy to receive social security benefits, to register as conscientious objectors if drafted for military service, and to sign marriage licenses.[44] Churches were granted protections for their property, tax exemption status similar to that of the Roman Catholic Church, and the right to collect and administer offerings.

In 2011 FEREDE published a statement calling the Spanish government to account for its failure to fully apply the laws of religious freedom for all confessions. They cited the censorship of public gatherings and inconsistencies in the granting of licenses to open churches or to have access to broadcast time on radio and television.[45] In 2014 they published a denunciation of the Spanish government's failure to ensure that all evangelical clergy were able to collect unemployment benefits for their eligible years in ministry prior to 1999. To support their complaint, they brought the situation before the European Tribunal of Human Rights, which ruled that the Spanish government had discriminated against these clergy based on religious motivations.[46] In a 2018 interview, FEREDE's Mariano Blázquez Burgo cited the example of Spanish income tax forms as evidence of remaining inequalities in religious liberties.[47] On the tax forms the only option for designating a portion of one's income as a religious donation was a box labeled "The Church." The Roman Catholic Church received all those monies; other faith communities were excluded. Faber names the privileged treatment of the Catholic hierarchy as evidence of lingering Francoist institutional continuity.[48] FEREDE's authority as the legal advocate of Spanish evangelicals is both a privilege of freedom and a necessary protection of that freedom.

Religious liberty was accompanied by another significant cultural shift: increasing numbers of migrants. Spain established its first immigration law in 1985 prior to entering the European Union.[49] Mario Izquerido,

---

43. Carlos, "Ley 24/1992," 3.

44. Prior to this, evangelical weddings were not recognized as legal unions before the state.

45. FEREDE, "Manifesto por la libertad religiosa," 2.

46. FEREDE, "Pastores jubilados," para. 1–2.

47. Villascusa, "Nuevo auge," para 3–5.

48. Faber, *Exhuming Franco*, 49.

49. Martín et al., "Latin American Immigration," 819.

Juan F. Jimeno, and Aitor Lacuesta write, "Inflows increased steadily, from under 30 thousand per year in 1996 to 958 thousand in 2007, when foreigners amounted to more than 12% of the total population."[50] Emma Martín Díaz, Francisco Cuberos Gallardo, and Simone Castellani note a dramatic increase between 1999 and 2001:

> In the case of arrivals from Ecuador, these were of particular significance[,] . . . becoming the country's third largest migrant collective, only exceeded in number slightly by Moroccans and more recently by Romanians.[51]

Citizens from countries that Spain had previously colonized were able to enter as tourists for up to three months without a visa.[52] Martín et al. remark that migration sharply declined after Spain began requiring compulsory visas for those coming from designated Latin American countries.[53] Spain's National Institute of Statistics reports 1,135,397 immigrants from Latin American countries in the first six months of 2022.[54] Overall, their report documents the greatest increases in the numbers of nationals from Ukraine, Peru, and Colombia.

Even with reduced migration numbers, Latin Americans now represent the majority population of church attenders in many evangelical churches. José Pablo Sánchez writes,

> An important part of the growth of evangelical churches has been facilitated by immigration that represents, in many congregations, 68% of the members, as is the case in Madrid. It is a new strength that is fortifying the development of a Spanish evangelistic movement. Nonetheless, the great challenge is to continue to grow in a special way among the indigenous population that continues to be very rooted in the culture of the past.[55]

A shared language, however, does not mean that the immigrants have integrated seamlessly into Spanish society and culture. FEREDE member Mariano Blázquez Burgo affirmed the role of immigrants in the growth of the Protestant church, yet added a qualifying observation: "Many of them

---

50. Izquierdo et al., "Spain," 6.
51. Martín et al., "Latin American Immigration," 822.
52. Martín et al., "Latin American Immigration," 820.
53. Martín et al., "Latin American Immigration," 822.
54. "Cifras de Población," 3.
55. Sánchez, "Drama de la España," para. 4.

prefer to establish their own congregations instead of integrating into existing ones."[56] However, there are two sides to this contextual issue, with the other being the perspective of Spaniards towards these immigrants.[57] Spaniards observe national, ethnic, and even linguistic diversity. This is not unlike the linguistic differences that English speakers encounter when speaking with English speakers from other countries. Martín et al. critique the validity of the "cultural compatibility" argument as being the primary factor for Spain's preference in admitting Latin American immigrants. These people, they say, represent a necessary work force in Spain who will accept low-paying employment, such as domestic service and agricultural work. Martín et al. write, "The workers of Latin American origin, in as much as they are integrated into the more precarious and less skilled labor markets, are as desirable as they are exploitable."[58]

If this applies to practices and attitudes in the context of Spain's labor and economy, it is possible that it might carry over into relationships among Latin Americans and Spaniards who worship together in the same faith community. The new majority Latin American population in the sanctuary may be family in Christ, but they are not ethnic Spaniards. The challenges ahead for Spain's Protestant churches will be twofold; first, as noted by Sánchez, they will need to find ways to reach out to and reintegrate indigenous Spaniards into the Protestant churches, those who "are rooted in the culture of the past."[59] Secondly, indigenous Spanish believers may need to honestly evaluate their own attitudes and actions for signs of discriminatory prejudice. They have an opportunity to redeem their own past experiences of discrimination by offering the validation and acceptance to Latin American or other ethnicities that they themselves had lacked for so many years in their own country. Even as issues of the past may be processed through critical remembering, the current social context continues to change.

In the twenty-first century, the pursuit of new liberties continues to characterize the decisions of the government and its people. Under Franco's regime, the nation was compelled to adhere to Catholic doctrine and practices. However, new laws on abortion, marriage, and euthanasia reflect an intentional rejection of former religious influences in the nation's political and social policies. In 2007–8, Spain was particularly

56. Villascusa, "Nuevo auge," 46–48.
57. Montañés, "Interacciones entre cultura(s)," 23.
58. Martín et al., "Latin American Immigration," 830.
59. Sánchez, "Drama de la España," para. 4.

impacted by the global economic crash. The country's optimism was abruptly checked. Severe austerity measures were enacted to prevent total financial collapse. The corporate suffering experienced by the population provoked the rise of the *Indignados* (Outraged), or 15-M, movement in May 2011.[60] Through the use of social media, people of all ages and social backgrounds came together to protest and demand change. The grounds for their grievances were a 20 percent unemployment rate, political corruption, merciless evictions of people from their homes, cuts to social spending, Spain's limited two-party political system, and the government's treatment of the banks. The protests produced dramatic change, including the rise of three new political parties and a redistribution of the balance of power in the government. The unity of the country shows signs of interprovincial differences as regional languages—for example, Catalan—are being taught in public schools and permitted for official use. In 2017 the province of Cataluña defied the seat of government in Madrid by holding a referendum on independence for Cataluña. And in 2020–22, along with the rest of the world, Spain endured severe lockdowns and high COVID mortality rates. Spain has experienced continuous change: political, social, economic, religious, and cultural. The minority Protestant community finds itself carried along in the current of transitions. This is their present contextual reality, yet, as this brief historical overview affirms, their present context is still highly impacted by their past.

Spain's Relationship with Faith, 1993–2019: A Statistical Picture

One of the ways that religious practice and faith can be measured or represented is through numbers and percentages. Spain's Centro de Investigaciones Sociológicas (CIS) is an autonomous organization that systematically conducts professional surveys to collect data about Spain's population.[61] CIS gathers data on demographics, behavioral patterns, and opinions on a wide range of topics: for example, the economy, politics, health, beliefs, and religion. The results are digitally published and freely available to the public. A second faith-based organization, Evangelismo al Fondo (EVAF), also collects statistical data on the number of Protestant believers and churches in Spain. It has produced reports for the years 1993, 1997, 2012, and 2019. For consistency and comparison with numbers gathered from

60. Feenstra, "Reivindicación de la ética," 14–16.
61. CIS, "Funciones," para. 1.

both sources, tables 1, 2, 3, and 4 use numbers from both sources but only from the years that EVAF produced reports.

CIS monitors Spain's religious affiliations. In the following table, the percentage of those who identify themselves as Catholics, whether they are practicing or nonpracticing, has decreased 19 percent in the twenty-six-year period from 1993 to 2019. The combined increase of those who identify as either indifferent or as atheist has increased by nearly 18 percent. There has been a 2 percent increase in those who identify themselves with another religion. Faith affiliation has steadily declined.

Table 1: Faith Affiliation in Spain, 1993–2019[62]

Date	1993	1997	2012	2019
Spain population	39,360,766	40,489,098	47,265,321	46,733,038
Catholics*	86.3%	81.9%	71.0%	67.3%
Other religion	.8%	1.3%	2.1%	2.7%
Indifferent^	7.6%	12.3%	16.5%	17.2%
Atheist	3.5%	2.6%	8.5%	11.8%
Missing	1.9%	2.0%	1.9%	1.0%
No. of respondents	2502	2492	2480	4804

* Percentage of Catholics: Total of those marking Catholic, including Catholic nonpracticing.

^ Percentage of indifferent: Total of those marking either indifferent, not a believer, or agnostic.

CIS inquires into the frequency of people's attendance in a church worship service. There was a 37 percent increase in those who rarely to never attend worship between 1993 and 2019. The declines in religious affiliation and participation are consistent with the results stated by Paul Tromp, Anna Pless, and Dick Houtmann in their analysis of twenty European countries. In their research, Spain and Belgium exhibited the greatest overall decline in their "traditional religiosity." Spain was one of

62. The numbers for Spain's population are from Álvarez, "Estadística total España." Information for 1993 is from CIS, "Barómetro de febrero 1993," q. 47. The information for 1997 is from CIS, "Barómetro de diciembre," q. 32. The information for 2012 is from "Distribuciones marginales," q. 29. The information for 2019 is from CIS, "Barómetro de diciembre 2019," q. C12.

three countries in which individuals reported experiences or feelings of decreased connection with their former faith.[63] Antonio Montañes notes, however, that there are examples across Spain of significant participation in local Catholic practices and religious festivals, for example celebrations honoring saints and romerias (religious pilgrimages).[64]

Table 2: Frequency of Attendance in Worship, 1993–2019[65]

Dates	1993	1997	2012	2019
Almost never	27.3%	45.1%	58.9%	64.2%
Few times a year	30.1%	18.3%	14.9%	14.7%
Once a month	13.5%	12.2%	9.5%	14.7%
Every Sunday	23.4%	21.1%	13.9%	7.3%
During the week	2.3%	2.8%	1.8%	1.5%
Missing	3.2%	.5%	1.0%	1.5%
No. of respondents	2502	2256	1814	3362

Every ten years, CIS conducts a survey that is more specifically focused on religious belief and practice. They inquire into parental faith background and include Judaism in the options, but Judaism is notably absent in the provided options for one's current religious affiliation. Those who select "Protestant" are asked to further specify if they are "evangelist," "Anglican," or "other." This is an example—in a government sponsored organization—of incorrect usage of the term "evangelical."

---

63. Tromp et al., "Believing without Belonging," 522.

64. Montañés, "Interacciones entre cultura(s)," 6.

65. Information for 1993 is from CIS, "Barómetro de febrero 1993," q. 48. The information for 1997 is from CIS, "Barómetro de diciembre," q. 32a. The information for 2012 is from CIS, "Distribuciones marginales," q. 29a. The information for 2019 is from CIS, "Barómetro de diciembre 2019," q. C12a.

Table 3: Distribution of Non-Catholic Faiths in Spain, 1998–2018[66]

Dates	1998	2008	2018
Protestant	30.0%	18.5%	32.5%
Christian	5.0% Christian Metaphysic*	2.2%	4.9%
Jehovah Witness	30.0%		5.6%
Muslim	20.0%	31.9%	26.6%
Buddhist	5.0%	3.8%	7.2%
Orthodox		16.8%	19.2%
Metaphysic/Spiritualist* church	5.0% Spiritualist Church*		
Missing	5.0%	26.9%^	2.0%
Total interviewed	20	97	109

* The 1998 survey included two options that do not appear in the later surveys: Christian Metaphysic and Spiritualist Church. No description of these two religions was provided.

^ The % of missing or invalid responses in 2008 was extremely high.

The data in tables 1 and 2 has significant implications for theological education in Spain. Overall, faith is declining; unbelief and disinterest are rising. Participation in worship has also decreased. According to the CIS data, the faith community with the greatest increase in numbers is Muslim, followed by Orthodox and Protestant. The low number of participants who answered this question on non-Catholic faiths is indicative of the minority status of these faiths in Spain.

The CIS data on evangelicals is incomplete and limited in scope due to its lack of direct contact with the wider evangelical community. EVAF addresses this gap, collecting statistical data on evangelical churches and the numbers of evangelical believers. Máximo Álvarez Álvelo, the director of EVAF, consults the various government statistical databases as well as data from FEREDE. Álvarez states that his organization collects their data through direct contact with sources, churches, pastors, and other

66. The information for 1998 is from CIS, "Religión," q. 50a. The information for 2008 is from CIS, "Religión (II)," q. 55a. The information for 2018 is from CIS, "Redes Sociales," q. 90a.

evangelical organizations to verify its reliability.[67] EVAF's data indicates steady growth in the number of churches and believers. In their 2019 chronological report on the growth of evangelical churches, EVAF reports the existence of fifty-two churches at the close of the nineteenth century, a number that increased to 3,915 by 2019.[68] The greatest increase took place between 2000 and 2010, when 1,301 new churches were opened. The following table uses EVAF's data on evangelical believers to establish their percentage within Spain's population.

Table 4: EVAF Data on Evangelical Believers in Spain, 1998–2019[69]

Dates	1993	1997	2012	2019
No. of overall population	39,360,766	40,489,098	47,265,321	46,733,038
No. of evangelical believers	74,312	86,841	319,721	382,436
Percent of evangelical believers to overall population	.18%	.21%	.67%	.81%
No. of churches	1,435	1,632	3,549	3,915

Though illuminating, these numbers fail to provide the demographic information on gender, nationality, ethnicity, or age. Consequently, they only provide a general picture of the numbers of people participating in the churches. The increase between 1997 and 2012 corresponds with a period of increased immigration to Spain, suggesting a correlation. Despite growth, this data confirms that the evangelical population is still very much a minority community in Spain.

The following table shows EVAF's statistical data on Protestants in Madrid, where the fieldwork for this research was conducted. The distribution of the number of people attending individual churches is not indicated in this data. Dividing the number of reported believers by the number of churches, this data suggests that each church would have approximately 192 members. However, the reality is that few evangelical churches have over one hundred in attendance nor do their physical structures or locations have sufficient space to accommodate 192 people. This suggests a gap in the data

67. Álvarez, email message to researcher, Nov. 13, 2017.
68. Álvarez, "España," slide 3.
69. Álvarez, "Estadística total España."

and possibly a discrepancy between the numbers of members on the church rolls and the number of people who actually attend services.

Table 5: EVAF Data on Protestant Community of Madrid, 1993–2019[70]

Years	1993	1997	2012	2019
No. of inhabitants	5,030,958	5,181,659	6,498,560	6,466,996
No. of Protestant believers	12,428	13,233	92,783	95,609
Percent of population	.25%	.25%	1.42%	1.48%
No. of churches	165	189	558	499

The data in tables 4 and 5 suggests several items for reflection. The implication of increasing numbers of believers and churches is that there is a need for increasing numbers of pastors and ministry leaders. However, the evangelical population continues to represent a small minority within the overall population of Spain. This, too, is the current reality. Seminaries are presented with the challenge of equipping more people for a faith community that struggles with marginalization, limited resources, and identity issues.

Dialoguing with the history of Spain's Protestant evangelical community has highlighted significant historically rooted, contextually based themes. Their influence extends to present attitudes and practices, including memories of oppression, marginalization, minority status, legitimacy, identity, and tensions and shifts between traditionalism and liberalism. New themes have risen out of the liberty made possible by Spain's transition to democracy: a context of continuous change, immigration and its cultural impact on Spain's evangelical faith community, and the overall societal shift away from its traditional faith heritage. These realities challenge theological institutions and the church to practice a cultural hermeneutic in their discernment of how, where, and with whom to contextually engage. Seminaries will need to evaluate their current curricular designs and practices to determine if they effectively equip students to trans-formatively minister in a context of spiritual decline. The seminaries and believers of Spain's evangelical faith community live and function within all these themes: those they have inherited, those that are contemporary, and those which await in the future as society continues to change. To design theological

---

70. Álvarez, "Estadística total España."

education contextually suited for Spain's evangelical faith community will require acknowledgment of, reflection on, and response to these themes. Contextualization holds the experiences and practices of the past together with the realities and trends of the present.

Questions for Reflection

1. What are two or three historical experiences of Spain's Protestants that are distinctive from or like the historical experiences of believers where you serve in theological education? What are the implications of those distinctives or similarities in your present context?
2. How can Scripture and the practice of critical remembering inform our present theological response to historical persecution and marginalization?
3. What are the recurring themes in the narratives told in the churches and in the theological institutions where you serve? To what extent have those themes been shaped by the historical and cultural context? How do those themes or narratives need to be contextualized to facilitate the mission of theological education or of the church in the future?

4

The Faith Community's Perspectives on Theological Education

To gain relatively reliable knowledge we need to rely on the interpretive skills of the entire community.

—Don S. Browning[1]

THE VOICE OF THE laity has often been absent in the academic literature of theological education.[2] Although the church's creeds affirm the unity of its body, its component parts tend to self-segregate: clergy and laity, elders and deacons, and members and nonmembers. With segregation, one group can be excluded. In the case of theological education, when the "for whom" continuum shifts to a select group, many individuals do not have access to the richness of theological formation. The survey "Perspectives on Theological Education" invited all church attenders in the province of Madrid to contribute their perspectives regardless of their previous knowledge or experience

---

1. Browning, *Fundamental Practical Theology*, 51.

2. The following are two examples: (1) Cannell writes, "One conclusion from the debate is that theological education is valid only if the community is broadened to include the church. In such a community of faith, theologians and church leaders become partners in the task of theology." Cannell initially calls for the involvement of the church in the theological education conversation but then restricts theology to the domain of ministry leaders. Cannell, *Theological Education Matters*, 271. (2) Martin Dowson and Dennis McInerney, researchers in Australia, note the lack of data from laity in theological education research and acknowledge the gap created by that absence in the comprehensiveness of the research results. Dowson and McInerney, "Theological Colleges," 404.

with theological education. To orient participants to the subject of the survey, the phrase "theological education" was briefly defined in the survey introduction as "education for people in ministry and church leadership as well as education for those who want to learn more about God."[3] The survey was structured so that people might gather clues about theological education from the context and flow of the questions. According to Sharon L. Miller, Barbara G. Wheeler, and Elizabeth Lynn, a perception study can be utilized to assess a local faith community's understanding of theological education and to provide a "basis in reality" to which institutions can then respond.[4] The discovery of congregants' perspectives on theological education was a critical aim for the validity of this work and to provide the seminaries with an updated and more comprehensive "basis in reality."

Listening to the Faith Community through a Survey

"Perspectives on Theological Education" was circulated in Madrid's Protestant evangelical faith communities from winter 2017 through spring 2018. Ministry leaders were given hard copies to distribute to parishioners, and shareable digital links facilitated additional access to the survey. The voluntary and anonymous participation of eighty individuals produced a rich set of quantitative and qualitative data. The survey had two aims:

1. To formulate a comprehensive description of the participants' experiences and understanding of theological education based on their responses. The questions explored participants' experiences and perceptions of their relationship with theological education and whether theology or theological education had a role in their day-to-day lives.

2. To identify possible influences or factors that contributed to the formation of their perspectives. The questions probed participants' opinions and invited their original contributions on how theological education should serve the church and equip ministry leaders.

---

3. During the development of the survey, I was asked if laity would understand the phrase "theological education." Although I noted Earl Babbie's caution that using unfamiliar words or phrases could affect survey reliability, I made a deliberate decision to use the phrase trusting that people would understand or gather enough information in the survey introduction to decide if they felt comfortable participating. Babbie, *Survey Research Methods*, 133.

4. Miller et al., *Making Connections*, 1.

The Survey Population

Nearly equal numbers of men and women participated in the survey, with ages ranging from eighteen to over eighty and three quarters of the respondents between ages thirty-five and sixty-five. Most were originally from Spain, an interesting result considering the changing demographic reality of Spain's Protestant churches.[5] The majority indicated a Protestant or Roman Catholic family faith background. None had backgrounds in Islam, Judaism, or Eastern religions. If this sample is representative, Spain's Protestant evangelical community is primarily composed of those with roots in Christianity. Most of the survey population had eleven or more years of involvement in Protestant churches and more than half frequently participated in worship services, Sunday School, prayer meetings, or midweek Bible studies. When asked to select titles that best characterize their roles in the church, the four predominant titles were: member (62 percent), teacher (54 percent), musician (22 percent), and pastor (18 percent).[6] Most had multiple roles in the church they attended, and only one person selected "pastor" as his/her only title. Those who chose to "speak" through the survey were experienced church people, highly engaged in a diverse range of activities. Twelve different denominational groups participated. Their denominational affiliations reflected a broad range of Protestant evangelical perspectives, ranging from historic European denominations, such as Anglican, Reformed, or Brethren Assembly, to the Pentecostal Church of Philadelphia, with its origins in Spain's Roma community. The group with the greatest representation attended nondenominational evangelical churches.

Those who had significantly less representation in the outcomes were newer congregants, recent converts, the youngest and eldest generations, and non-Spanish members. These would be important groups to include in any subsequent research; their voices could add nuances and perspectives that might clarify, emphasize, or qualify the outcomes of this study. Overall, the survey population were seasoned, indigenous, active Protestant evangelicals. The breadth and duration of their experiences and knowledge provided the foundation for the four themes and five perspectives that emerged from their responses.

---

5. Regions represented by respondents were Spain, Central America, South America, North America, Europe, and Africa.

6. The survey "Perspectives on Theological Education" is provided in appendix 2.

Perspectives on Theological Education

The survey collected respondents' perspectives and opinions on theological education from several different angles. Most questions provided options from which people could select the answer that best represented their experience or perspective. Ten free-text open questions were interspersed throughout the survey to collect qualitative data and to give people an opportunity to express their opinions. Answering questions was not required for completion of the survey. Their original contributions were substantial and intentionally given.

Perspectives on the Purpose and Founders of Theological Education

The majority affirmed that a university degree is highly valued by Spanish society and that pastors and ministry leaders need some type of specialized education. Overall, they expressed strong support for an educated clergy who are formed either in the academy or through in-ministry settings such as the local church. They were nearly equally divided in their opinions about who was primarily responsible for the establishment of the seminaries, choosing between Spanish or missionary founders—an interesting result, considering that Protestantism was introduced to Spain primarily by foreigners and that many of Spain's evangelical seminaries and Bible institutes were initiated through missionary partnership. This result indicates that there is recognition of the missionary impact on theological education, yet it is balanced with an awareness of, and perhaps pride in, the current significant indigenous presence in many seminary faculties. The overall majority affirmed that theological education's primary objectives, ranked from highest to lowest percentage, are to serve the church, equip people to communicate their faith, prepare students to serve the needs of society, provide resources to inform daily decisions, and equip people to practice personal faith. Their responses expressed a comprehensive aim for theological education that includes three contexts of ministry: the church, society, and the individual.

Perspectives on Qualities and Skills Needed for Ministry Leadership

The next series of questions asked which qualities and skills were important for ministry leaders to have or to develop. The section included the first free-text response. Seminaries can utilize these results to evaluate whether their design and practices are intentionally cultivating these qualities and skills in their students.[7]

Table 6: Qualities and Skills Needed for Ministry Leadership

Qualities and Skills	Ranking
Moral integrity	3.92
Spiritual giftedness	3.81
Provide pastoral care	3.75
Theological and biblical knowledge	3.69
Effectiveness training new leaders	3.55
Visionary leader	3.49
Flexible	3.48
Committed to evangelism and missions	3.41
Self-assured	3.23
Ability to work with all ages	3.16
Dynamic preaching	3.10
Active in social justice	2.82
Administrative skills	2.69

These rankings offer a contextually generated list of congregational expectations for ministry leaders. Moral and spiritual formation are prioritized, with pastoral skills and biblical knowledge closely following in importance. Although social justice ranked lower in this series, in subsequent questions, the participants expressed concern for effective societal

7. Participants rated the importance of each quality or skill using a four-point scale where a score of four indicated high importance and a score of one, low importance. The total number of points for each quality and skill were tallied and the computation of the mean provided an average rating for each item.

engagement. This was the first of three occurrences in which preaching and administration ranked in the lower third of importance—a result that I had not anticipated.

Those who took the opportunity to write in additional qualities and skills prioritized the importance of ministry leaders' character and virtue. They cited humility, or a synonym of it, most frequently—for example, "to lead with a towel on one's arm."[8] One participant substantiated the significance of an exemplary life: "[The] life [of a leader] must be such that others can copy it without danger." Several suggested qualities and skills for pastoral care, emphasizing love and empathy. They specified that pastoral caregivers be "hospitable," "know how to listen," and "know how to communicate." They elaborated on pastoral effectiveness in training others: "[to have an] ability to work in a team and with teams." The need for teams, creating them or working alongside them, was repeated throughout the survey as well as their desire to have leaders who are able and committed to empowering others. One comment succinctly stated the reason for the emphasis on teamwork: "No one is valid for everything; a leader needs others." Through their statements, the survey participants reflected a vision of the church as a community of purposefully engaged individuals. The implications of their perspectives on relational and empowering leadership call seminaries to reflect on the leadership that they model and how they are equipping their students to lead others. Participants also introduced the new recurring topic of the necessity of ministry leaders who understand the societal context of labor, who "know the working world."

Perspectives on Three Core Characteristics of Theological Education

Next, three multiple choice questions explored the participants' understanding of the phrase "theological education" utilizing three of the four continua: *for whom, location in relation to church and society,* and *aim or purpose.* The majority, 60 percent, indicated that theological education is for "all believers," twice as many as those who chose clergy or "the called." It is important to note that no one selected "for no one." The results indicate a high degree of receptivity to theological education and its pertinence for all believers. Although "seminary" was chosen as the most effective location for theological education by 41 percent of respondents, "anywhere" followed with

---

8. An allusion to John 13:3–17.

30 percent and the "church" with 18 percent. The range of responses suggests an openness to a diversity of educational contexts. Finally, a majority, 61 percent, indicated that the primary aim of theological education should be the development of "theological and biblical understanding." Fewer, 20 percent and 16 percent respectively, selected the development of "spiritual maturity" and "practical skills for ministry." This result was unexpected. The church has sometimes been associated with a narrative that portrays academic theological formation as an ivory tower, out-of-touch with daily life. Also, some trends in ministry formation have prioritized practical training. Summarizing the results of the answers to these three questions, most of the participants envision theological education that is for all the church (for whom), that could be locationally accessible even if offered on a seminary campus (location), and that its purpose (aim) is to theologically and biblically form ministry leaders, while not neglecting the development of their devotional lives and practical skills for ministry.

Perspectives on Responsibilities of Theological Education

This section concluded with three sets of questions that specifically investigated the participants' expectations of theological education's responsibilities. Each section included a final open response question. First, they ranked the importance of six types of formation.

Table 7: Formation to Be Facilitated by Theological Education

Formation in:	Ranking
Biblical and theological understanding	3.82
Personal integrity	3.66
Personal spirituality	3.64
Ability to reflect theologically about life and society	3.53
Lifelong learning	3.46
Leadership	3.32

They prioritized biblical and theological understanding slightly over personal integrity and personal spirituality. These three types of formation were consistently valued by the survey population. In the open responses, two comments shed light on the low ranking for leadership: "I do not believe in leadership, but rather in service[,] . . . [how to be] faithful and dedicated servants." Another wrote: "In the evangelical church, [they] hardly know this concept [of authority], and when they know it, it is almost always deformed." They suggested the need for formation that teaches "[how to respond] to the challenges posed by society," "how to contextualize the [gospel] message for actuality," and "how to practice your faith during your day-to-day work," the recurring topic of integrating faith in the workplace. Several commented on the importance of facilitating the formation of relationally astute leaders who can "work in a team, [have the] capacity to delegate," "learn to encourage others," and "[know] how to love." One unique suggestion for relational formation stood out for its practicality, specificness, and theological implications for Christian hospitality: "I seriously propose, [sic] formation in culinary skills. I think that in all seminar[ies] there should be a course to learn to cook and all the virtues of the fellowship of the table."

In the second grouping of questions, participants ranked the abilities and practices that they expect theological education to nurture in its students. Note the low ranking of administration.

Table 8: Abilities and Practices to Be Developed through Theological Education

Abilities and Practices	Ranking
To practice theological reflection in all aspects of life	3.69
To provide pastoral care	3.66
To teach	3.59
To train and equip others	3.55
To evangelize	3.44
To serve the local community	3.44
To preach	3.41
To practice spiritual disciplines such as prayer and fasting	3.25
To minister to children and youth	3.19
To administrate	3.16

Although fewer contributed open responses, the ability to form a team was again emphasized: "care for the team, like delegate." Three specific abilities were mentioned for the first time: "to identify the false doctrines that attack the church," and "to help those with physical limitations," and "[to give] talks about different topics for the congregation and the family." These suggestions give contextual information to seminaries about issues that are of concern to congregants.

The final items to rank were twenty-five courses, a list primarily based on the curricula of several theological schools in Madrid with a diverse range of both theoretical and applied courses.[9]

Table 9: Ranking of Most Important Courses Taught by Theological Educators

Courses	Ranking
New Testament	3.8
Pastoral Care	3.8
Marriage and Family	3.7
Old Testament	3.7
Christian Ethics	3.6
The Trinity: God, Son, and Spirit	3.6
Theology	3.5
Youth Ministry	3.5
Apologetics, Defending the Faith	3.5
Evangelism and Missions	3.4
Spiritual formation, Such as Prayer and Fasting	3.4
Methods for Effective Teaching	3.4
Science and Faith	3.3
Spiritual Warfare	3.3
History of the Reformation	3.3
Church History	3.3

9. "History of the Reformation" was included specifically because the survey was distributed during the year of the quincentenary anniversary of the Reformation, initiated in October 1517 in Germany by Martin Luther.

Courses	Ranking
Social Justice	3.3
Church Planting	3.3
Preaching	3.3
Eschatology, the Study of the "End-Times"	3.2
Church Administration	3.0
Worship	3.0
Biblical languages, Greek and Hebrew	2.8
World Religions	2.8
Philosophy	2.7

Theological and biblical knowledge, pastoral care, and courses facilitating relational engagement were again prioritized. Courses that equip ministry leaders to serve particular social and spiritual needs were interspersed throughout the top two-thirds of the rankings: marriage, youth, and spiritual formation. Preaching and administration ranked in the lower third. The placement of worship was unexpected. Music and singing saturate the culture of Spain as well as its churches. Although participants were not asked to give reasons for their rankings, their contributions to the open response question to suggest additional courses, provided insights into the courses that they think are critical for ministry leaders in Spain.

Some of their suggested courses were courses on postmodernism, social pedagogy, general sociology, social psychology, and "social assistance in the community." "It is OK to study about the history of the church, reformation, philosophy, but [one] should look forward, [to] how society is evolving and how to evangelize a society more polarized economically and more corrupt." One suggested course, "Introduction to the Working Life," represented the recurring concern for lived faith in the context of daily labor. Two recommendations addressed training needed to serve distinct demographics: "The Evangelism of Children" and "Care of Elderly People." Outliers, like these last two examples, speak loudly due to their uniqueness in the data.

Hermeneutics was specifically suggested by five different people, which was particularly interesting considering preaching's consistently lower ranking. One stated reason for proposing hermeneutics was "to teach the Bible with biblical balance in all topics... to [avoid an] exaggerated emphasis in spiritual warfare that many teach." It seems reasonable to assume that preaching is not devalued, but that this group recognizes it as one of the ways that the church communicates with its people and the local community.

Team work was mentioned again: "One person does not need to know everything. It is better to work with a team." A concern for balanced formation through mentorships was also suggested: "More than additional theoretical materials, I see as important that one includes practice that could include the experience of other pastors, mission[aries] or evangelists. The example is worth much." Finally, there was a subject mentioned that had been absent until this point in the data: "the 'mother' Catholic church." Although there are other major religious groups in Spain, there was little indication of a concern to know more about those faiths. Their vision or conception of theological education is of formation that equips the whole person to serve knowledgeably, skillfully, and with integrity inside and outside of the church.

The Relationship Between the Church and Theological Education

The survey inquired into the relationship participants and their local churches have had with theological education. Participants were first asked to write how their church equips its people for ministry. According to their statements, the churches in Madrid offer a variety of formational activities: Sunday school, Bible study, classes, and seminars. Several mentioned discipleship but did not specify how they define it nor how it is practiced in their church. Some mentioned opportunities to study with formal institutions. Concern for effective engagement with the local society motivated one church to train its people: "They teach them in a practical form to know the culture in which they move, and later how to act supporting friendship, care, and empathy towards the people with whom we are surrounded in a continuous or spontaneous way." Only two people cited preaching as a means of formation.

In contrast to these positive comments, 21 percent wrote that their church either does not equip people or does it poorly or without intentionality. One wrote: "Very sadly [my church] does not equip, I studied and formed myself because I enjoy knowing the Word." Another shared that the faith community nurtures itself: "Mutual care . . . no one has been equipped." A few gave reasons for the lack of training: "[The church] doesn't consider theological training." "With the previous pastor, there was pastoring of leaders, but not mentoring. With the most recent changes, there is nothing." In contrast, one noted a problem with training saturation: "It is hardly done because we have 'more than enough' seminarians and formed people with experience." No one wrote that training was unneeded or unwanted, only that it was not offered in their churches.

The second question was, What helps people to follow Christ in today's society? Most frequently cited were reading the Bible and formative personal relationships, including family, mentors, pastors, other believers, and even those in society: "Sharing life with others is what makes me understand how to be more like Christ." One person compared pastors to "mirrors to look at to serve Christ in this society." Another found inspiration from "the excluded and [those] in danger of exclusion. The poor and marginalized." Less frequently cited were Christian literature or digital resources. Several also indicated spiritual sources of help, including Jesus Christ, the Spirit, personal faith, prayer, Holy Communion, and meditation: "In my mind, [there is] an image of Jesus on the cross, taking my evil by washing me with his very clean blood." Although they learn from others, the participants were actively engaged in their own spiritual development.

Next, a series of questions gave participants a list of options from which to choose. The section concluded with another open response question that invited them to describe how theological education institutions engage with their churches. The majority indicated that their pastor has theological education; it was a fact known to the congregants. All indicated that they knew at least one person who had done theological studies. Theological education is neither unfamiliar nor distant; it has a personal association with a face and a name. A majority, 82 percent, indicated that a seminary faculty member speaks at least once annually in their churches. The 35 percent who selected "weekly" may have pastors who work bi-vocationally as seminary professors. Few, 11 percent, indicated that faculty "never" speak in their churches. Those who made this statement represented multiple denominations, some of which have seminaries in Spain. Half reported that informational materials about theological institutions were posted in their churches. The data indicates that Spanish theological institutions do advertise their programs in some local churches, and some churches post that material when they receive it. The majority, 63 percent, affirmed the existence of either a financial or student-sending relationship between their church and a theological institution. However, more than a third indicated that their church does not or that they do not know if it supports a seminary.

When asked about the geographic proximity of a seminary or Bible institute with which the church has a relationship, 30 percent indicated that the question did not apply to their churches. This was, however, nearly the same percentage of those who were unsure if their church sends students or financially supports a seminary. The next most frequently selected location, 22 percent, were seminaries in other provinces. Three of the five civilly accredited Spanish Protestant seminaries are located outside of the province of Madrid, which may account for that ranking. If the percentage of those who indicated that their church is involved with seminaries located in the province of Madrid, 16 percent, is combined with the percentage of local in-house church programs, 15 percent, then 31 percent of the churches represented in the survey sample are supporting programs within the province of Madrid. The number of online students, 1 percent, was likely significantly altered during the pandemic, from 2020–21, when many institutions had to transition their instruction to digital delivery.

Another open response question asked people to write how theological education engaged with their church. Only a small group wrote that they did not know. Those who answered affirmatively reported five forms of involvement. First, a seminary equips those sent by the church to study: "Equipping those who go and from that the church benefits because they are better prepared." Second, the seminaries send their students to practice and serve in the churches: "Our church chooses a seminarian which is a blessing for everyone." Third, several wrote that the seminaries send personnel to speak at events such as evangelistic campaigns. Fourth, the seminaries have provided relational, direct support through in-person training within some of the churches: "It uses our building to give classes, and that is how we know it and various members attend it." Another wrote: "Our church formed in the center of [a seminary], our pastors also were formed in the same, and we have constant contact with the seminary." Fifth, in at least one instance, the institution assists the church financially: "[The seminary gives] voluntary offerings to supplement the expenses of the building where the church meets." Based on their responses, when a relationship exists, it is a symbiotic relationship that benefits the church and the institution. The implication for theological institutions is the value of proactively developing relationships with churches, including physically sending faculty or students to churches to incarnationally represent that relationship.

A final series of questions investigated the participants proactive engagement with theological education. Most respondents, 75 percent, have viewed a seminary web page. Although they were not asked to give their reasons for searching, this indicates a level of interest in these institutions, an awareness of the seminary's digital presence, and a population that is active online. The number who had visited a campus, 77 percent, was slightly greater than the number who had visited web pages. They were not asked where or why they had visited these institutions, but these results indicate a high level of familiarity and experiential knowledge of the institutions. Two-thirds had some type of prior experience with theological studies, and of that group, 45 percent had completed a theological course of study, receiving a certificate, diploma, or degree. Nearly a quarter of the survey population was actively pursuing theological formation, academic and applied, whether through opportunities to take one course, earn a certificate, or to enroll in a formal tertiary program of theological education. What is not known from the data is whether these percentages of engagement with theological education are representative of the overall Protestant community in Madrid or whether participants were drawn to the survey because of a previous interest in the area. The invitation to participate in the survey specifically stated that it was to be distributed to parishioners. No previous experience with theological education was expected or requested. This was also stated in the introductory paragraph of the survey itself. It is possible that the survey population may represent a minority group within the wider Protestant evangelical community of Madrid.

The penultimate free-text question asked participants how their studies had contributed to their lives. Most of their comments testified to the ongoing benefits they reap from their studies: "Almost every day something happens that causes me to think about something that I learned during the years of my theological studies." Some mentioned the personal value of studying, such as "helping me to understand myself as a person, as a believer, as a pastor, and helping me to understand the religious dimension of a person." Several commented on increased knowledge of the Scriptures, that theological study "stimulates the abilities to investigate the Scriptures." Others, likely those with ministry responsibilities, focused on the impact of their studies in the areas of preaching and teaching, including "better comprehension of the Word and help in the preaching of it, as well as to impart classes in the church." Another participant noted that "the knowledge of the Bible helps you to understand many necessary concepts in order to have a doctrine and an experience of the faith. You need this to be able to transmit to others that it really is worth the trouble to believe in a God like ours."

They reported their appreciation for how theological formation had facilitated their empathetic relational formation: "In the way I relate with others, now it is always intentional, and I try to encourage them in whatever way is possible." Another wrote, "There were classes in counseling, and it helped me to know how to understand and care for the people that I helped." One comment, however, was particularly negative: "They are very superficial courses. They don't support much." This person provided some context for this critique in the final open response of the survey, addressing me directly: "A warm greeting. A faithful agnostic." For whatever reason, although agnostic, this person chose to engage in a survey about evangelical theological education. The implications for theological education are that it bears fruit in the personal lives of its students and equips them with knowledge and skills to serve others in the context of ecclesial and social communities. What is important to note is that the survey was not distributed to former seminary students but to parishioners. This aligns with this work's definition of theological education as formation for all the church.

An Open Invitation to Contribute Their Own Perspectives

The final question invited participants to share anything that they thought should be added to the data collected through the survey. The most prevalent theme in these concluding comments was accessibility: "I believe every believer should have a theological education adequate to his/her level and gifts." Another specified that this accessibility should be an aspect of weekly worship: "It does not have to be something 'special' to go to a biblical center, but rather something integral to the worship and part of the 'routine' of Sundays. The negative of this is that in many cases it remains in the Sundays and does not end up being a part of every day to day." They further qualified accessibility as availability: "The seminary should come closer to the local churches, with the purpose of preparing more of the members to serve better." Others commented that it should be accessible for all educational levels, offered online, and advertised: "It would be important to facilitate where and how we can have this theological formation." Another writes, "I believe that, in general, they should advertise Biblical studies more and clarify for believers that all who study are not necessarily to be [a] Pastor afterwards."

They made suggestions about the practices of theological institutions, recommending that they be "empathetic" and "unconditionally liberating." "A seminary should be neither exclusively 'pietistic' (only devotional teaching) nor exclusively academic (only philosophical-theological formal teaching.)" Respondents wrote about the responsibility of theological education to equip and empower students: "[Theological education] should teach people how to think [critically]." One said, "[It should] develop practical and vital models of discipleship." They specifically commented on theological education's role in leadership development: "[Pastors should be taught] to preach in an adequate manner, without exaggerated emotions, loudness, nor exaggerated gesticulations." Furthering this point, one participant writes, "Another important topic is to prepare them well for leadership because I have seen much abuse of power, spiritual abuse, and many people do not know how to work in a team, and they consider the church to be their property." One participant offered a constructive suggestion for the development of pastoral leaders, a model that could be applied both to an institution as well as the local church:

> The need of a mentor to whom [you can] be accountable and who supports you in prayer and pastoral [care]. In Spain, I believe, this is something that we lack and for this many of us need to go [along] trying things when someone could have oriented us. It is too bad, but God teaches us that the elder men teach the young men and the elder women teach the younger women, and to me this is mentorship and discipleship, necessary for personal spiritual growth and for the growth of the church in our country.

Five respondents touched on contextualization and theological education's role to engage with society. One suggested additional coursework on contextually situated topics rooted in Spain's historic Roman Catholicism, including "teachings about the mother of Jesus, confession not only before God, [and] the Deuterocanonical books." This was another of the infrequent references to Roman Catholicism, a noteworthy detail. Another wrote: "[Theological education] should be oriented to . . . influence the society and the culture, achieve that it would be more just and less hostile to Christianity." In the context of their concern for society, two alluded indirectly to the "ivory tower" narrative: "I would like for theological education to focus more on the practical needs that the world today is living and how to help it and not to be making speculations about biblical passages that only brings discussion and confusion among believers." Another wrote,

> In many theological schools they end up creating academic theologians, but [they are] boring, distanced from [what] society is actually asking, or incapable of connecting with it.... We should be capable to use theology in a practical way ... to lift up and open the mind to reflection. To not simply vomit what has been learned. One supposes that we can learn how to reach [those outside of the church], not distance ourselves from them by our academic bubble and cusp.

Finally, one person specifically addressed the critical importance of contextualized theological education:

> There should be programs that have been born in Spain by Spaniards. If a program does not utilize Spanish professors, it is not valid today. The missionaries can help, support, but not do everything. Programs from American megachurches ... cause more damage than help.... They bring a different culture, not the Word.

In summary, they envisioned theological education that is accessible to the faith community, that practices relational theological formation, and that is thoroughly contextualized in all aspects to address the real and situated concerns of the people in the churches and society. Participants interacted with the survey statements by contributing additional insights, illustrations, and applications. Several suggested items that they believed had been missed and some addressed the researcher directly. Through their contributions, they exhibited a high level of personal subjective engagement with the survey. They expected that the researcher would "listen" to what they wanted to say.

The Fruits of Listening to a Faith Community's Survey Contributions

Four Overarching Themes

Four overarching themes were woven through the expressed perspectives of the survey participants. The first theme was virtue, based on the participants' recurring emphasis on the possession, cultivation, and exercise of integrity in those who are theologically trained for ministry leadership. An implication of this theme for theological education is the importance of *paideia*, intentional facilitation of character formation. The second was *acompañamiento*—to accompany, or as expressed in the survey, to work and walk alongside of parishioners.[10] This theme is grounded in their numerous statements of expected relational competencies for ministry leaders—leaders who nurture and equip the faith community to serve together within the contexts of the church and society.[11] Interpersonal relational engagement characterized their expectation of ministry leaders as well as how they wanted to be equipped to interact with the society. The third theme, knowledge, encompasses the necessary academic course work or experiential education that participants expected theological education to deliver in order to equip ministry leaders with tools for theological reflection and discernment. They want knowledgeable leaders who can offer practical wisdom for life and ministry. Finally, the fourth theme was personal spirituality, expressed through their recurring references to ministry leaders' devotional practices and relationship with God.

Based on these four themes, the data could be summarized as follows: *Congregants expect theological education to equip and form ministry leaders who are people of virtuous character, who serve and empower the church to engage with society through skilled empathetic relational abilities, who practice holistic lifelong learning and theological reflection, and who attend to their personal spirituality.*

Five Perspectives and their Implications for Theological Education

The survey's title communicated its fundamental aim: to discover the faith community's perspectives on theological education. Five perspectives emerged from the participants' contributions. These perspectives have significant implications for the designs and practices of theological education in Spain and, through correlation with the designs and practices of theological education, in other contexts as well.

First, the responses of the participants reveal their perspective that theological and biblical knowledge are necessary components in the

10. The noun *acompañamiento* and verb *acompañar* were repeatedly cited in the data.
11. Forms of *acompañamiento* recurred throughout the data.

formation of ministry leaders. Importantly, they clarified this perspective through repeated variations of statements to stress that the transference of that knowledge from faculty to student is not sufficient in itself. The participants expressed an expectation that ministry leaders are to be practiced in the application of that knowledge through theological reflection to lead the faith community as it grapples with the challenges and adjustments produced by a continuously changing society. One might have expected the respondents to prioritize practical in-ministry experiences over the acquisition of academic theological knowledge, but consistently throughout the data this knowledge was viewed as essential for a leader's preparation. Based on this perception, the implication for the design and practices of theological education is that it would integrate the acquisition of knowledge and the practice of theological reflection into all aspects of its theological, biblical, and applied ministry formation.

Second, the responses of the participants reveal their perspectives that theological formation is to be holistic and balanced, integrating experiential practice with knowledge and character formation. The ministry practices that they prioritized were relational abilities and *acompañamiento*, such as empathy and interpersonal team-building skills, rather than clerical skills like preaching, serving sacraments, or administration. The participants suggested the incorporation of the practices of discipleship, apprenticeship, and mentorship to provide contexts and opportunities to develop empathetic and nurturing interpersonal skills. The implementation of these suggestions would facilitate the formation of safe spaces for a student's personal spiritual development and character formation in the context of small supportive discipleship communities. The implication of this vision of holistic formation for the design and practices of theological education is that it would develop a plan of studies designed to form relational, reflective practitioners.

Third, the responses of the participants reveal their perspective that ministry leaders should be equipped to facilitate the development of a participatory community of believers. The survey results did not support expectations of a do-it-all ministry leader but rather one who is committed to corporate ministry and who has a humble, moral, virtuous character. The theology of leadership emerging from the analysis of the collective data is characterized by leadership that comes alongside of others, *acompañamiento*, to equip and care for them and to then serve together in the contexts of society in which they find themselves. The design implications of this emphasis challenge theological education institutions to review the theology of leadership that they are teaching and/or modeling through all aspects of their curricula: the taught, null, and hidden curricula.[12] A commitment to this type of formation comes with a caveat: the responsibility of confronting and perhaps redirecting away from ministry those who exhibit do-it-all tendencies or moral weaknesses that would predispose them to stumble or wound others. This will require institutions to evaluate their commitments to fulfil this critical role of assessment and to work in partnership with the church for the sake of the entire faith community, including their students and themselves.

Fourth, the responses of the participants reveal their perspective that theological education should be accessible to everyone in the church. Significantly absent from the majority of the data was a perception that theological education is detached from the life of the community of faith. The implication of this perspective of theological education is that the formation of the entire community of faith should inform and guide the development of theological education's design and practices as it considers its relationship with local churches and the society. Whether they open their doors to the community of faith or take formation to the churches, it will be critical to equip ministry leaders with a vision and understanding of learning theories and tools to effectively pass along the education and practices they have learned to the people and to intentionally cultivate leaders characterized by humility, love, and empathy.

Fifth, the responses of the participants reveal their perspective that the community of faith needs to remain theologically faithful as it engages and serves the non-confessing society. Although Protestants represent a minority population in Spain, it was significant that isolationism was not put forth as an option in the data. The implication for theological education is that it should expand the scope of its course of study beyond the interests of the church to include engagement with the society and its needs and questions. By practicing and modeling theological reflection that directly engages with societal trends, the faculty can equip ministry leaders to simultaneously maintain both faithfulness and relevance without fear as they respond to non-confessing ideologies. These ministry leaders can then model and teach this practice to the community of faith,

---

12. These are descriptions of what is intentionally taught, what is learned from what is missing (null), and what is being taught but not explicitly stated as such. See Shaw, *Transforming Theological Education*, 79–90.

enabling it to fulfil the desire expressed in this data to both witness to and serve the local community.

Questions for Reflection

1. What surprises you about the perspectives, opinions, and vision of theological education shared by this faith community? What ideas or critiques concerning your own context were inspired by their comments? Give two or three examples.

2. How do you listen to the community of faith in your context? What are your expectations of their ability to provide constructive contextual information about theological education? Write five to ten questions about theological education that you would like to ask the people in your local churches.

3. How would you evaluate the applicability of the five perspectives and their related implications for your own context? If you were to act on one of the implications for theological education, which would you choose? What concerns, weakness, or goals would it help you to address? How would you implement it in your context?

5

Listening to Three Seminary Communities

> *As I work on another transcription today, I am embarrassed as I listen to myself ask questions. Sometimes I am struggling with the Spanish. I would get nervous and then stumble over words, even when they were sometimes on my paper. But even [during] the English interviews, especially with a Spanish speaker, my thinking was taking place in two languages at the same time, so it's obvious, especially to me, that I am struggling to put together clear, concise questions. I feel, in response, especially grateful for the hospitality and graciousness of those who were interviewed. They have things that they wanted and want to say, so they, I believe, were willing to speak with me in spite of my stumbling with words. I think that they somehow understood or sensed that I was genuinely interested, and so they spoke.*
>
> —Colleen Weaver[1]

THE RESEARCH FOCUS NOW turns from the perspectives of the people attending churches to the theological institutions that serve them. The seminaries' designs and practices are probed to examine and reflect on their contextual awareness and responsiveness. The data reveals the particular and real situation of each seminary. Faculty and student perspectives

---

1. Colleen Weaver, coding reflections journal, May 9, 2019.

highlight multiple interconnected contextual dynamics that anchor, guide, challenge, and critique theological education. Six themes emerged through the process of careful listening: context, mission and identity, contextualization of the curriculum, accreditation, church relations, and societal engagement. Although these themes are explored separately, they are inter-connected, representing the complex holistic structure and function of each seminary. Each case study concludes with a graphic representation of how that institution answers the four continua questions: For whom is theological education designed? Which educational methodology is utilized? What is the purpose and aim? Where does the seminary location itself in relation to the church?

An Overview of the Three Seminaries

In May 2018, I conducted case studies in three distinct Protestant evangelical seminaries in the province of Madrid, Spain.[2] Within the Protestant community of Madrid, these three seminaries would be identifiable due to their denominational distinctives and to the relatively small size of Spain's Protestant community. Although they signed consent forms allowing disclosure of the institutional name, I have chosen to refer to them simply as seminary A, seminary B, and seminary C. Their anonymity focuses the analysis on their distinct approaches to theological education.

The case studies included faculty and student interviews, campus visits, and a review of institutional documents and related literature.[3] Each seminary is affiliated with a distinct denomination. Faculty members,

---

2. For my research, I chose seminaries that are physically located in Madrid and offer their instruction from Madrid either in person or digitally. I contacted two additional seminaries but did not receive a reply. I did not contact seminaries in other provinces, nor did I include seminaries that have a learning center in Madrid but are based out of a geographic location other than Madrid.

3. Before I completed the final analysis of this data, the COVID-19 pandemic had dramatically impacted human interactions, particularly in fields like education where in-person communication has often been a primary mode of instruction. Although seminary B's degree program was previously delivered exclusively online, all three seminaries had to adapt their programming to comply with government lockdowns and social distancing regulations as evidenced by announcements on their websites. The scope of long-term consequences resulting from the pandemic extends beyond the framework of this research, but the likelihood of adjustments in some of their practices since the case studies were conducted, such as the mode of delivery and course offerings, is highly probable.

generally but not exclusively, are affiliated with the founding denominations. The institutions accept students from diverse denominational and faith backgrounds. The number of matriculated participating students in each seminary varied between approximately twenty to fifty, although with quite different full-time equivalencies (FTE).[4] The rector at seminary A explained the contextual reality for Spain's evangelical seminary enrollment expectations: "We have students, but we always want to have more. . . . The number of students [in all of Spain's seminaries] is in direct relation proportionally to what is the reality of our churches." Seminary A's students are typically full time; it is primarily a residential seminary. Seminary B's program is online; nearly all students are part time. Seminaries A and B have full-time and part-time faculty. Seminary C meets in person, once per month, seven months out of the year. Student attendance rates vary from month to month. All faculty and students at seminary C are part time.

Although the three institutions include international faculty, each is led by a Spaniard and has a majority of Spanish faculty. Of the ten faculty members interviewed, nine were Spaniards and one was an American; five have earned doctorates. Of the students interviewed, 60 percent were Spaniards; additional nations represented were Peru, Brazil, Venezuela, and an unspecified "Spanish colony." The overall percentage of women and men interviewed was 40 and 60 percent respectively.

Seminary A

The Context

The Historical Context

Since its 1922 founding in Barcelona, primarily by Baptist missionaries from the United States, seminary A has faced intermittent challenges. It was closed from 1929 to 1948 due to financial limitations, a side effect of the Great Depression.[5] After reopening in 1949, still under foreign missionary leadership, it continued its educational ministry in Barcelona until 1976 when denominational leaders decided to relocate to the province of Madrid. The seminary had persevered through the Francoist regime,

---

4. The FTE of each seminary is different based on its schedule and platform of course offerings.

5. UEBE Facultad de Teología, "Dossier informativo," 3–4.

1939–75, a period when religious freedoms for non-Roman Catholics were greatly restricted. In 1978, the seminary installed its first Spanish rector and has had continuous Spanish leadership for over forty years. In the 1990s, it began to admit students from other denominations and initiated its distance program of theological studies.[6] The seminary is registered with FEREDE, the official Protestant legal organization that has advocated for Spanish Protestants since 1986. Through FEREDE's advocacy, seminary A received national accreditation in 2011.

The Physical Context

The decision to purchase undeveloped land just north of Madrid's city limits, the centrally located capital of Spain, was based on the expectation that the seminary would then be accessible to all Spanish provinces.[7] Over the last forty years the town where seminary A is located, has nearly doubled in population.[8] Newly constructed high-rise apartments and businesses now surround the campus, and a commuter train station within a block of the seminary provides direct transportation into Madrid.[9]

The seminary grounds are bordered with fencing and privacy shrubbery that enclose a playing field, picnic area, parking, and the modest three-story seminary building that holds classrooms, offices, a chapel, a library with over twelve thousand volumes, and student apartments. Now surrounded by the bustling metropolis, class bells regulate the rhythm of the seminary community on this land that is both academy and home to its residential students. The campus design suggests that the original and current intention is to provide a somewhat cloistered context for residential students—the monastery model.

---

6. Díaz, "40 años," para. 6.

7. UEBE Facultad de Teología, "Dossier informativo," 4.

8. Population census from 1981 to 2021. Brinkhoff, "Alcobendas in Madrid (Madrid)."

9. I lived in the town where the seminary is located from 1995 to 1998. At that time, the seminary sat as a solitary building on the town's edge, and buses were the only means of public transportation to Madrid. The train and subway lines that connect the town to Madrid have greatly facilitated the town's growth.

The Residential Community

Several students highlighted the formative impact of their residential experience even though they were not specifically questioned about it. The residential community provides them with an environment of mutual support, a forum for the discussion of ideas, and the promise of lifelong professional friendships. For student A-4, the campus community has been a significant catalyst for personal change during her seminary experience: "Regarding the experiences with [classmates], the moments of being able to read together, of sharing doubts, insecurities, fears . . . [about] ministry, that's what has most been important to me in this course." Another student (A-7) said that living at the seminary helps him "more than anything" with the challenges of studying. A further student (A-10) commented that living in the residential community has fortified his sense of vocational identity. This protects him when he leaves campus:

> It marks much, much, much, much the difference [between] . . . not being here and . . . being here. . . . We can take advantage of the time. But I see it more as strengthening what we are doing. When I leave this door, I don't feel the danger . . . that I am going to contaminate myself with what I am going to see or what I am doing or with whom I am doing it. . . . To live here situates me in myself, in my sense of calling and the purpose for coming.

One student (A-9) however spoke more critically saying that living on campus "disconnects [him] from the social reality for four years. . . . It isolates us a little." He relies on some of the faculty to "feed us . . . [as] they are in the churches, of the movements they see, of what is happening and how we will have to respond."

González writes, "In its initial use, a seminary was a seedbed. In a garden, the main purpose of a seedbed is to keep young plants in a protective environment."[10] When exiting the campus, student A-10 is not afraid of "contamination" from whatever or whoever is outside. His comments suggest a perceived us versus them dichotomy between those within the residential community and those outside it. As a seedbed, the campus is a safe place of fellowship for students, but it is also disconnected from the community that surrounds it. In the context of the campus design, these comments suggest the influence of a hidden curriculum. Shaw writes, "A hidden curriculum often trains our students in the exact opposite way to

---

10. González, *History of Theological Education*, 122–23.

that which we teach in our explicit curriculum and claim in our purpose statements."[11] The seminary is affiliated with a mission-oriented church-planting denomination. Faculty A-12 notes: "[Our aim] encompass[es] everything that is included in the field of mission[,] . . . *very* missionary" (emphasis original). Yet, the unofficial ethos of the residential setting, perceived by some students as an insulated protective environment, may inadvertently run counter to the seminary's taught and stated model of missional and contextual engagement, at least regarding the surrounding non-confessing community. In the most recent version of seminary A's website, one of five primary informational tabs is: "Residence: Live with Us in the Faculty."[12] The residential component is central to their physical as well as formational context.

In his review of theological education, Banks acknowledges that a residential design patterns Jesus's practice of asking men and women to come away from their present lives for a dedicated time of study and development.[13] However, Banks also argues for the necessity of incorporating Jesus's example of going out to engage with the local community.[14] Seminary A's campus serves as a ministry staging area from which students are sent out to required ministry placements in local churches.[15] Their accreditation documents state, "To these [students] should be given the opportunity to put into practice the theoretical knowledge gained in class in the context of service in the church and in the society, providing them with supervised activities of a practical character by pastors-professors of proven experience."[16] Although their 2021–2022 Dossier Informativo includes the possibility of placement in either churches or "collaborating entities," the stated aim for students is "the formation . . . of aptitudes for ministry, particularly for pastoral service."[17] I found no list of community or societal placement options, such as hospitals, prisons, or rehabilitation centers; however, employment in those societal contexts is listed as a future possibility for those who earn the bachelors of theology degree.[18] Prioritizing

11. Shaw, *Transforming Theological Education*, 81.
12. "Reside con nosotros en la facultad."
13. Banks, *Reenvisioning Theological Education*, 94–126.
14. Banks, *Reenvisioning Theological Education*, 106, 111.
15. UEBE Facultad de Teología, "Dossier informativo," 35–37.
16. UEBE Facultad de Teología, "Memoria del título," 14.
17. UEBE Facultad de Teología, "Dossier informativo," 35–36.
18. "Grado en teología," para. 4.

ecclesial contexts for ministry practice limits students' exposure to the wider society, and, in particular, to their local neighborhoods. The practice of separation from society, although a characteristic of the monastery model, can subtly instruct students as a hidden curriculum.

Mission and Identity

The Significance of Vocation

Each faculty member stated the seminary's mission succinctly and without hesitation. Rector A rooted it in the seminary's historical context.

> It is the same purpose from when it was founded in the year 1922, being an institution of theological education, our purpose is to prepare workers, ministers of the gospel[,] . . . that they would have an academic theological formation, but we greatly emphasize . . . pastoral vocation and the service to others.

The students' responses affirm that seminary A uses the term vocation in its original Latin meaning, "a calling." When asked to give their motivation for studying, all but one student referenced a divine call as the stimulus for their theological pursuits. Student A-1, for example, said, "What I felt was that God was calling me to prepare myself and to serve him in a specific form as a pastor, evangelist, and missionary." Vocational formation for ecclesial ministry anchors and frames the seminary's mission.

The Course of Study

The seminary offers three residential programs of theological study: accredited bachelor's and master's degrees and an institutional diploma. They also offer a certificate for those studying in their extension program. The bachelor's degree in theology aims to equip pastors or ministers to serve the church in today's society.[19] The postgraduate degree offers advanced academic and professional formation in theology and requires knowledge of English to facilitate access to a wider range of academic resources.[20] The third program, an institutional diploma trains people who either do not

---

19. The bachelor's degree is 240 ECTS, the master's degree is 60 ECTS, and the diploma is 180 ECTS. "Grado en teología," para. 4.
20. UEBE Facultad de Teología, "Dossier informativo," 10.

meet governmental entrance requirements for the accredited program or who choose that option. The diploma course also "equips [people] for ecclesial service."[21] Additionally, they offer an institutionally designed distance program in theological formation that aims (1) "to harmonize theological education with the needs of the evangelical work in Spain, preparing workers and leaders for diverse ministries in the church"; and (2) "to decentralize the education so that it can reach a greater number of people."[22]

Recent regional Spanish independence movements and other societal shifts such as the pandemic and economic stresses have influenced peoples' ability and/or willingness to relocate or to commit to residential study. The distance program may become an increasingly attractive option for its online accessibility.[23] However, this will necessitate a paradigm shift away from reliance on the residential program. Other than one student (A-5) who mentioned previously studying in the distance program due to work and family obligations, faculty A-13 was the only other person to refer to the distance studies. From all indications, the residential campus and its activities have been the primary hub from which formation and resources flow. The existence of the nonaccredited extension program indicates receptivity towards contextualized adaptation to serve churches. However, the interview data, now reenforced by the current version of seminary A's website, which highlights living in residence, suggests that remote learning is not considered as high value in comparison with residential formation.

Academic Identity

Seminary A's level of academic professionalism is a significant component of its institutional identity, noted in the repeated references to its academic qualifications in several interviews. Rector A stated, "We are a theological institution of modest dimensions, very dignified, within the evangelical camp of Spain, very recognized, but modest." Student A-9 commented, that the people at the seminary "sacrifice themselves. . . . Their names could shine in other places and they decided to invest their lives here."

21. "Diploma en estudios teológicos," para. 1.
22. "Teológica a distancia," para. 4.
23. Some of those shifts are represented in the demand for and accessibility of competitive online options, the prohibitive economic implications of relocation and full-time study, and changing student demographics—evidenced in increased numbers of nontraditional students, women, and diversity due to immigration.

Even though she expressed some dissatisfaction with a lack of depth in her theological studies, student A-4 said, "I chose the best cloister there was in Spain. And in these times, that's here."

Perceived Threats to Their Mission and Identity

Seminary A is facing two challenges that threaten its ability to fulfil its mission and maintain its identity. They represent obstacles to overcome as well as possibilities for future contextualization and institutional health. The tenacity of its confident assurance becomes evident when set against the context of what it perceives as its most serious challenge, the scarcity of resources. Financial limitations impact its ability to fulfil its educational aspirations. Faculty A-12 noted,

> There is no money. Clearly, there are many projects, but the resources are few. . . . It would be interesting to have more[,] . . . more personnel, but that is impossible for us. The library . . . needs more investments, because today all the information [technology] resources . . . cost a lot of money.

Seminary A receives an annual contribution from the denomination but no assistance from sources outside of Spain. It experiences scarcity in the number of personnel. Rector A acknowledged, "There are *few people* to do so many things. Because the economic resources are also limited and those who serve here try to cover all of these necessities" (emphasis original). To help ease the financial burden of the seminary, Rector A said, "The faculty nourish themselves with their personal resources," testifying to their sacrificial vocational commitment.

The faculty quietly nourish the students as well, and remarkably, the students have no or little knowledge of the faculty's economic sacrifices. When asked how the seminary supports them in their studies, student A-10 shared, "It relaxes me to know, that . . . if in any moment that I cannot pay, I can be tranquil. I will be able to continue. . . . The faculty desires that I be formed." Similarly, student A-8 said, "They had patience with me paying. . . . The truth is in the economic sense they have supported me and helped me." Student A-1 talked about his unexpected scholarship:

> They have helped me, above all, economically. For example, I received scholarships that I did not expect. Suddenly I arrive with my two cents, and they tell me that you have something here. They

have given me as an institution and as professors in an individual form . . . [an anonymous financial gift].

Personal financial sacrifice has been a practice of the seminary, a community ethos of commitment to sustain the institution. Yet, the culture is changing. In her concluding comments, faculty A-12 said,

> I would like that the people who are called by God would be willing to leave their social situation, their work[,] . . . to dedicate themselves to prepare to work for the Lord . . . even though their finances will be much worse. . . . Today the youth study, careers, they have good positions. And later [they] have to denounce all this [for ministry]. I, my desire is . . . that they desire to dedicate themselves to the Lord even though their finances will be much worse.

Changes in student attitudes towards money and financial loyalties reflect contextually situated trends rooted in the current economic experiences of Spain's seminary students, churches, and society. Financial scarcity may remain a constant challenge; however, financial sustainability, outside of unlimited endowments, will demand ongoing contextual adaptation amidst variable circumstances and generational attitudes and practices regarding personal resources.

Demographic adjustments in the student population have transformed and continue to challenge the seminary's identity. When faculty A-12 came with her husband in 1986 to study at the seminary, accepting women as full-time students was not the practice. She shared her story:

> When I came to the seminary, [the administration] did not want to allow me to study because I was to be the wife of the pastor, not the pastor. Therefore, I said [to them] what would happen, I could pass three years of my life here wasting time, or they could allow me to study. . . . And from there began to open a little a crack and [women] began to come.

Both this woman and the seminary took risks—she, by challenging the seminary to theologically reflect on the value of her theological formation as a pastor's wife, and the seminary, by expanding its practice to include female students.[24]

Civil accreditation obligates the seminary to implement nondiscriminatory enrollment practices. Seminary A complies but stipulates in the

---

24. Rector A made a point of noting their nondiscriminatory position towards women.

Dossier Informativo that it is preparing adults for ministry in Protestant denominations.[25] Rector A said,

> [Receiving civil accreditation] means that here people can study who do not have a vocation for ministry, but the majority continue having this characteristic because our character and our publicity always insist that, here, we want to form workers for the work of God.

Student A-5 described the challenges that a non-confessing student would face at the seminary: "If someone comes that doesn't have . . . that love of the Lord, the one that doesn't have it can't communicate, can't transmit, can't encourage another. . . . You have to come with it. . . . It's difficult to get here." Given that the institution is committed to missions, these comments reinforce the presence of a hidden curriculum on the segregated campus. Preservation of its historic identity and formational mission to equip people for ecclesial ministry are critical for its perseverance through chronic scarcity and required inclusivity.

The Contextualization of the Curriculum

According to Rector A, "[The seminary follows] a classical curriculum, more academic, inherited from the Anglo-Saxon, or European tradition," a legacy from its North American missionary founders. Spurgeon's College in London and Theologisches Seminar des Bundes Evangelisch in Germany also served as models for the seminary's curricular design.[26] Courses in the eight-semester bachelor's curriculum are grouped into four areas, the fourfold model critiqued by Farley: sacred Scriptures and biblical languages, history, theology, and pastoral studies. When asked how the curriculum's design was specifically adapted for the context of Spain, Rector A repeatedly referred to the 1922 founding date.

> [The original design] had much to do with the needs of the infant Baptist work in Spain because there were different churches rising up and they needed . . . pastors and . . . lay workers who from their work and professional commitments also [helped] to generate new points of mission. This was the original vision that has [been] maintained during the years.

25. UEBE Facultad de Teología, "Dossier informativo," 13–14.
26. UEBE Facultad de Teología, "Memoria del título," 10.

The aim of the original design, "to prepare workers [and] pastors with good formation," guided a revision of the curriculum and course content in 1996. The most recent revision took place in 2010–11 to comply with Spanish civil accreditation standards for universities. The seminary now submits to external evaluations by the accrediting agency but also, less formally, conducts its own internal evaluations. Rector A observed,

> We are in a moment when there is a demand that there be a revision, an evaluation of the effectiveness of the current plan of studies with respect to the results, if our graduates really have the profile that is needed to serve as pastors . . . in the churches. . . . Therefore, certainly we will soon begin a new curricular revision maintaining the courses that we have, but revising their content, incorporating, above all, all of the changes in theological education and in the actual society of the last few years.

He added, "We look to see if the students have acquired the knowledge and the tools that permit them to serve in a society like ours. It has changed, and it is still changing. . . . It is in process." What Rector A did not specify was the plan or process for conducting this evaluation. He said the seminary would continue with the current curriculum, but that they would make adjustments in course content. Limiting the projected means of contextualization to the selection of content could overlook other areas in need of revision, such as formational and spiritual practices, types of ministry practice placements, educational methodologies, administrative policies, and institutional societal engagement.

The contextual factors to which the seminary must respond are not only those presented by the church and the society. They must also respond to the challenge of generational differences within their student population. Rector A described some of the distinctive characteristics of the younger generation of students:

> The great challenge where we now find ourselves is our students, those who come, are every time younger. There was a time when a person came to the seminary who . . . already had life experience, of service in the church. . . . Now it is not like that. . . . They arrive, young students, some of them with vocation effectively, but they finish, still being very young, and they are not always prepared to be able to begin a pastoral ministry in the church. It has to do with the character. . . . There has been . . . a very great social change in Spain and other countries. And this generational change implies that the standards of maturity are not what we had before.

Rector A's recognition of the need to focus more on character development, or *paideia*, harkens to the Athens model of theological education. Finding a way to balance the seminary's current emphasis on professional and academic training, the Berlin model, with an emphasis on character formation presents a significant challenge. The answer, in part, may lie in their proposed student competencies, the development of which are required for civic accreditation.

The attitudinal competencies or section sub-labeled "BEING" in seminary A's accreditation document cites twenty-four character formation aims, but Rector A did not elaborate on these objectives.[27] Arguing for greater effectiveness in pastoral formation through a competency-based model as opposed to a traditional scholastic model, James K. Mwangi and Ben J. de Klerk state: "The competencies encompass the development of the whole person: affect, understanding, character, and skills."[28] The accrediting agency's requirement that institutions implement a competency-based model could be a key resource for responding to their acknowledged need to address student character formation.

In contrast to Rector A's observation that the seminary should be more intentional about cultivating character formation, the students reported practices within the institutional environment that have produced transformative change in their thinking, attitudes, and maturity. Student A-9 said,

> Regarding the training, it's very enriching to be able to contrast different points of view, further than what you consider biblical or by your own [previous] training, your own teaching from [your home] church, to be able to see the current diversity and [variety of] thought. . . . So, you also confront the reality that you could be wrong on something that you took as very sure.

---

27. For example, "estabilidad emocional [emotional stability]" (CEA6), "integridad personal [personal integrity]" (CEA7), "una sana estima propia y madurez personal [healthy self-esteem and personal maturity]" (CEA8), "simpatía y compasión [sympathy and compassion]" (CEA11), and "flexibilidad y apertura a nuevas ideas [flexibility and capacity to adapt to new ideas]" (CEA18). The document cites four categories of competencies: general, cognitive, instrumental, and attitudinal. All represent desired outcomes based on the study of theology and church ministry. UEBE Facultad de Teología, "Memoria del título," 17–22.

28. Mwangi and De Klerk, "Competency-Based Training Model," 6–7.

Student A-3 reported: "[Seminary] has also changed my perspective. A lot of things I didn't know. I had no idea. My parents had taught me. Now I am reviewing it." Student A-7 admitted,

> I came with a very closed imagination of what theological studying would be but I think that with the professors and everything they've helped us to be able to see different perspectives, not only the one we're accustomed to in the [denominational] churches here in Spain but also different perspectives and to evaluate it.

Student A-8 described the transformative impact of her studies.

> [Seminary] takes you to transforming well your view of seeing God, your way of seeing yourself, your way of you working in your life, of walking. . . . I suffered a crisis of faith, not regarding the existence of God but yes regarding rethinking many things that before you considered valid and now you rethink that maybe it's another way.

These students are experiencing unlearning, new learning, individual learning, and learning in the diversity of community. Their experiences challenge them to reevaluate their untested beliefs, assumptions, attitudes, and personal faith. Although the faculty may observe differing generational levels of maturity, the educational environment is facilitating student character formation. The contrast between the faculty and student perspectives on the degree of character formation taking place within the learning environment suggests a missing or insufficient protocol designed to monitor and evaluate the development of attitudinal competencies. Simply taking time to have conversations that prioritize listening to students could produce fruits of rich informative feedback.

The Role of the Faculty in Contextualization

Spanish faculty members are regarded as the primary agents for the contextualization of the curriculum. Faculty A-12 said,

> There have been periods when the teaching was more . . . brought from the United States and the context that functions there, but here in Spain at times [that] does not function. . . . We are adapting ourselves to see our form of being. . . . The majority of the professors are from Spain, although we have collaboration from the

United States. . . . We have a professor from South America . . . but the rest basically are Spaniards. Therefore, the context is similar.

Several students held the same opinion. Student A-3 said, "It is very good that it is a Spanish teacher that is teaching. . . . [It] gives you the perspective from someone that is inside." Student A-9 observed that not all of the faculty are equally skilled in contextual reflective practice. "Contextualization is in the hands of . . . the professors. And some of them . . . are very sensitive to what they see around them in the church and they inform us. Student A-6 focused on critical limitations in the transferability of this non-systematic approach.

> Maybe [it would be good to have] more time with tutors or pastors from here, not only the subject—that theory is very good and necessary—but to see how they have put it into practice. The professors know the Spanish society, they know because we talk about it, but it's not formalized in any subject or tutoring or practice mentorship. . . . Maybe spending time with a professor or someone who can help make that transfer of information [would be good].

This student's suggestion of a mentorship or apprenticeship model echoes the relational pastoral model repeated by those who participated in the congregational survey. Indigenous Spanish professors who are also practitioners, pastoring, or serving in leadership in local churches, represent an invaluable contextualization resource. However, a lack of intentionality in the transmission of the skills and understanding of contextual theological reflection methods could leave many students unprepared or ill-equipped to practice the discipline of cultural astuteness.

Rector A listed several societal developments that challenge the current design and formational status quo: "[There is] a complete social debate about the question of gender. . . . The phenomenon of immigration [is] so massive in Spain, and within this phenomenon the Muslim presence in Spain[,] . . . political participation [in context of] much political momentum[,] . . . . [and] ecology." He called these contemporary issues "elements of reflection." This reflective posture, although necessary, suggests that their response will likely be reactive rather than proactive. Rector A alluded to the existence of gaps in the current course of study that would have to be filled to address these societal shifts.

Student Perspectives on the Contextual Appropriateness of the Curriculum

Seminary A's students provided insights on the relevance of seminary A's curriculum and identified gaps in their formation. Their comments were constructive, thoughtful, and expressed their desire to prepare well for ministry within the diverse and changing context of Spain. Two lines of questioning were implemented to discover their perspectives on the actual contextualization of the curriculum.

The first line of questioning requested that students share types of formation that they consider necessary for effective ministry in Spain. The rapidity and concreteness of their responses exhibited a high level of cultural astuteness. They emphasized their need to know how to relate to and communicate with individuals and various social groupings such as families and different ages groups and ethnicities in the church and in society. Student A-11 elaborated on the need for instruction in family systems. Additional suggestions were psychology, pastoral counseling, and various forms of societal engagement, including "philosophy but in relationships." Student A-9 said, "I don't think we are at all prepared to . . . receive nor heal that which we are simply condemning"—in other words, to minister to people who may not be living according to the church's teaching.

Several students stressed the importance of developing their communication skills for effective engagement with the educated Spanish population. Student A-10, who is from a different Spanish speaking country, said, "I see so many ways to think, so many ways of living, so much culture, customs, to be able . . . to share the word and that it be listened to, it cannot be as I came doing it in my form," that is, the way he spoke with people about faith in his country. Student A-7 suggested equipping students with skills to make connections with people in their work place. "I think that it would be excellent . . . to have, apart from theology studies, like a complementary . . . secular profession. . . . Work with other people . . . opens a lot of doors in the sense of being able to give testimony." A theology of work was also a theme in the congregational survey data. Finally, two mentioned the importance of studying Spain's history. Student A-9 commented, "Being able . . . to have a more complete perspective of what has been the historical-social trajectory of Spain would be interesting. I think we aren't at all up to date. I think we're very behind the social changes that have occurred." Student A-1 said,

There is no history [course] for example of Spain and this is fundamental to be able to help them to know where they come from and where they are going. [Without this] you continue lost, in the sense of how to approach a Spaniard with the gospel. For this you have to know the Spanish culture not only of today but also of yesterday.

The second line of questioning asked students to suggest courses to add to the curriculum. Their suggestions primarily clustered into three categories: social sciences, biblical studies, and pastoral or applied theology. Under social sciences, they suggested psychology, family systems, sociology, and there was one mention each of worldviews, cultural context of Spain, ethics of culture, and conflict resolution. These areas of study would not typically be included in the fourfold design. Under biblical studies, they proposed biblical customs, geography, anthropology, history, and archaeology. In pastoral or applied theology, they would add apologetics, emphasizing the need to be an effective communicator in Spain. Student A-7 said, "We need to be prepared to be able to know what to respond, when to respond and in what way." This student also recommended adding two semesters of Christology as "an exclusive subject." He considered it to be basic "according to the context of Spain," perhaps a reference to Spain's historic Catholicism.

Finally, two foreign students, one a native Spanish speaker and the other from Brazil, suggested a course in *castellano*, Spain's Castilian Spanish. Student A-1 said, "Although I speak Spanish, in my country of origin—it is a Spanish colony—they speak *castellano* but it is different. People think it is all the same, but it is different [laughter]." Student A-3 voiced a similar frustration. "In Spain you have people from so many countries, but they all speak Spanish. So, it's complicated to talk with someone that doesn't have the same vocabulary as you. It's the same language.... But they don't speak the same way you do. ... For me the language is a big challenge." This contextually grounded critique highlights subtle yet critical differences among Spanish speakers. Considering the growing numbers of Latin American members in Spain's Protestant churches, these students have identified a cross-cultural skill that would enhance communication and promote the development of community among all Spanish speakers regardless of their countries of origin. Their comments indirectly critique reliance on the contextualization of course materials by indigenous faculty whose communication may be unclear to non-native Castilian Spanish speakers.

If courses were to be added, what would the students eliminate from the curriculum? This question elicited some discomfort; few responded. The students, in general, wanted more rather than less. Four would remove or reduce the number of history courses, particularly the history of the seminary's founding denomination. Two would eliminate a required course in choral music. According to student A-2, the choral course contributes to the concept of an "orchestra pastor," one that is expected to do everything. The "orchestra pastor" leadership model does not fit well with the current reality of Spain's bi-vocational pastors, neither does it harmonize with the relational empowering model generated by the survey participants.

The original course of study includes some courses, like choir, that are based on tradition rather than current trends and practices. Student A-1 said, "Hebrew is only symbolic because we do not have time to [study] deeply, therefore it remains in the air." Student A-9 expressed a similar opinion, but rather than delete Hebrew, he wanted more opportunity to study it. "We barely get enough to be able to read or translate. . . It's not sufficient to be converted into a tool." Students have perceived an inconsistency between the value that is rightly placed on knowing biblical languages and the limited amount of time allotted for language acquisition. The academic study of Hebrew has perhaps become disengaged from its vocational function as a tool for students to interpret and apply ancient texts for faithfulness in the society in which they live. Student A-4 addressed the impact of this issue throughout the curriculum: "The challenge is to forget the Bible because it's used very little in the classes . . . and another thing is how we believe that we're always talking about God. We don't take time ourselves with God." Contextualization of the curriculum includes the evaluation of its relevance, ministerial purpose, and life application for those who are to be educated.

Two students perceived a lack of interpersonal formation and suggested the incorporation of mentorships. Student A-4 commented,

> I think what's missing is a mentorship here. I think it's one of the things that's not here. . . Even though they might assign us a tutor [a requirement of the ministry placements], there isn't a true tutorial work, there isn't a follow-up. . . . I miss the ability to say, "Well, I have these doubts."

Student A-8 expressed a similar critique.

> Because of what the other students say . . . and because of what I [am experiencing], we are missing feeling taken care of more pastorally. I know that maybe it's not so curricular . . . but, yes, it's true that it's a special time where you're setting yourself apart, normally leaving family, job. . . . You're set apart, serving in churches that aren't yours, . . . and somehow, yes, we're missing a more pastoral labor. . . . I think it would be good to have a spiritual mentor of some sort, not only an academic tutor . . . that doesn't express much interest . . . in the student, but . . . spiritual mentors that are worried about how you are living because at the end you're not preparing as a mere professional, for a career. In that sense I think we feel a little alone.

Mentoring is a form of relational formation. The desire and vision of these students for this type of holistic interpersonal education was also voiced by church members in the survey. Mentorship that provides relational support, spiritual counsel, and ministry training is a model that Spanish believers, ministerial students, and church members value and want implemented in their contextualized formation.

The students highlighted their perceived need for more practical applied preparation. Student A-6 said, "I see there is a big jump from theory to practice in my ministry. . . . I think we will end up well trained, but how to use it? We don't know and we need to know." Student A-8 commented, "In general everything [needs to be] a little more practical. . . . A lot of things that we [are] supposed to know but the reality isn't so. . . . In other words, very practical things and here they don't teach that." Student A-9 mentioned being taught the complexities of ethics. "But [the application is] left to your own criteria and you'll confront it when you get there [to your ministry placement]. . . . We barely touch the edge of the mantle in all of these things." He acknowledged the serious implications of these perceived gaps in his formation.

> Although you have, very clear, a calling from God, you don't know either how it will be, nor where it will be, nor how you will deal with it, and also seeing all of the shortcomings you have, the insufficiency sometimes of what you expected of training—like we said before in ethical issues—or in how you'll carry it out. The fear grows at working with . . . lives and in God's work knowing that God will ask an accounting . . . of what we do with his work. So, of course, that fear is a great challenge but that is the fear more than completing an assignment.

The students' perceptions of deficiencies in their practical formation echo issues identified in Farley's critique of the theological encyclopedia design's outcomes, the fourfold design used by seminary A. Farley writes, "The students' and ministerial graduates' version is that the theological school did not adequately prepare them for the nitty-gritty problems and activities of churchly life, that the academic and practical were never really linked." The compartmentalization of the four disciplines does not facilitate their integration and application in theological reflection. If students fear that they will be unprepared to engage effectively with the people and situations of their ministry placements, they are perceiving that they are not learning or practicing how to problem-solve or how to theologically reflect and process situations that they may face in ministry. Seminary A's practice of placing students in ministry experiences throughout their degree program provides a curious backdrop to these comments on the perceived lack of practical formation. Students may be expecting the seminary to do for them what the seminary has designed for them to learn through self-discovery and actual experience. *Acompañamiento* seems to be desired and needed.

Regarding the pertinence of the course resources, such as textbooks and presentations, student A-10 expressed insightful concerns.

> The idea is, what I am looking for is, the relevance, and the power. . . . It has to do with the relevance of the education, that it is something of support. If it facilitates the students, it could arrive at equipping the people in the church . . . to touch and to reach people in the surrounding area.

Church Leadership and the Course of Study

To probe the contextualization processes from another angle, I asked the faculty if external groups had input or influence on the design and practices of the institution. Rector A reported,

> [When it comes to defining] the curriculum the executive council of the faculty has a much greater protagonist role. It is integrated with officials of our denomination, representatives of the pastoral collective. It is a diverse board. The local faculty is represented by the rector and the dean. Among everyone we try to integrate and generate a useful program.

> This executive council has the power to make necessary changes to adjust the curriculum *always* to the necessities of the churches. (Emphasis original.)

Direct involvement of the local church in curricular and program decisions, as evidenced through the composition of the executive council, is consistent with seminary A's vocational emphasis to equip women and men to serve the church. This relationship serves to help ground the seminary's academic pursuits in the life of the church. However, the relative absence of references to student or lay input in the interviews may indicate the presence of another hidden curriculum on leadership and authority. The present structure and power of the council may unintentionally model for students a preference for a hierarchical decision-making structure. This could set a precedence for students' future engagement in communities where they will serve—a leadership style that would conflict with the relational leadership suggested by the members of Madrid's faith communities who participated in the survey.

Seminary A's administration recognizes that society continues to evolve, that those changes impact the church, and consequently, their vocational formation should be adjusted to equip their students for present and future contextual mission. Historical consistency rather than an ongoing process of contextualization has primarily characterized their design and practice during the first one hundred years. The suggested outcomes-based assessment of "look[ing] to see if the students have acquired the knowledge and the tools that permit them to serve in a society like ours" indicates a degree of change—readiness in response to the immediate context. It will be critical to move from intention to implementation. The student interviews offered specific recommendations for contextualized formation for effective ministry in contemporary Spain. They also suggested the implementation of either mentorship or apprenticeship models; this generation longs for relational investment. With only one student representative on the executive council, the student input into the institutional design and practices may be quite limited.

Accreditation

Accreditation by an external validating authority requires compliance with established standards of performance, organization, and transparency. Recognition that an institution has fulfilled and maintains its relationship with a local accrediting body represents one form of contextualization. Seminary A is one of five Protestant seminaries accredited in 2011 by Spanish civil authorities, specifically the National Agency of Quality Evaluation and Accreditation (ANECA).[29] To obtain that status, the seminaries worked under the advisement of the FEREDE, which provided legal advocacy. Through this process, the seminaries adapted their courses of study to comply with the norms of the Bologna Process.[30] The rectors of the five accredited seminaries partnered under the guidance of the FEREDE to form the Commission for the Accreditation of Centers and (Academic) Titles of Protestant Theology to establish and uphold standards for theological and academic excellence for Protestant seminaries seeking civil accreditation.[31] This collaboration is ongoing. A seminary dean, who participated in the initial cohort of the commission, said, "With the approval of the Royal Decree on the eleventh of November 2011, the [Protestants] of Spain reached another great historical vindication of recognition of their fundamental rights."[32] For Protestant seminaries in Spain, civil accreditation signified a high level of academic achievement and educational professionalism and, perhaps more importantly, a victory in their struggle for genuine religious liberty and equality.

The Costs of Compliance

Compliance with ANECA's standards required adjustments in course design, sacrificial dedication of time, and evaluation conducted by an outside governing body. Earning civil recognition required years of planning and adjustments. Rector A described the process and how their historical identity and mission anchored them through it.

> We had to do a new design, but we tried *to maintain in essence* what we had before because we understood that the revision that we did in 1996 obeyed that purpose and *we maintained that purpose*, so

---

29. ANECA was founded in 2001. It is a full member of the European Association for Quality Assurance in Higher Education (ENQA) and the International Network for Quality Assurance Agencies in Higher Education (INQAAHE). It is also listed in the European Quality Assurance Registrar for Higher Education (EQAR). "ANECA," para. 1–2, 5.

30. "Se constituye formalmente la Comisión," para. 1–2.

31. "El Gobierno español aprueba," para. 1, 4, 12, 15.

32. "La titulación de los centros," para. 6.

> we incorporated new courses, but we *maintained in essence* what we had defined in the decade of the nineties, giving it a content that was perhaps better, more demanding. (Emphasis added.)

The seminary undergoes external review by ANECA every four years. Rector A explained, "What [ANECA] look[s] at are the results, the graduates, they look on the basis of the competencies.... We establish competencies for each course. The state evaluates if we have fulfilled this goal." He further described the accreditation relationship: "They [ANECA] do not interpose so much in the content but rather they check us to see if we are doing what we have said [we would do]." The verbal phrase "do not interpose" implies the existence of boundaries, areas that are off-limits. They are committed to their historic purpose and to their liberty to select the instructional content. Student A-9 voiced the only negative critique about consequences of the new design:

> So as an institution with [its] face to the government . . . it gives me the sensation that what's being sought [by the seminary] is surviving within the legislation, so [ANECA] won't take [away] our degree, the recognition. . . . The shortcoming . . . exists when sometimes we prioritize the academic . . . with lectures, work. . . . We could take more advantage in those inspirational times that could also be more contextualized [with more practical application]. . . . So now that we are more [of an accredited] faculty, it seems that the application [of the course materials is neglected]. . . . Because now we are an institution . . . that teaches because it's what the state asks, right? . . . But we miss it a lot.

The pressure to maintain high academic standards, in this student's opinion, limits time given to theological reflection and application to concrete ministry experiences. Maintaining a constructive formational balance between theory and praxis will be an ongoing challenge as the faculty navigates between accreditation requirements and its vocational aims.

Faculty A-12 spoke of the personal sacrifices that the staff had to make to become an accredited institution: "[Accreditation] has been . . . a very long and very expensive project, not financially but expensive in the [amount of] work and effort. Because we are a seminary, we have very few personnel and therefore, we have had to extend our hours in an extraordinary manner." Even though accreditation has been costly, two students specifically stated that it was a factor in their decision to enroll in the seminary. Faculty A-12 shared that Rector A understands the value of access to an accredited Protestant theological degree in Spain because he had to earn his theological degree in South America. "In Spain, at that time, [the accredited degree] didn't exist."

Challenges and Opportunities with Civil Accreditation

ANECA requires seminary A to regularly gather evaluative data from students, faculty, support staff, employers, and graduates.[33] The survey data is collected and reviewed by a quality committee composed of faculty and a student representative.[34] Student A-1 mentioned his utilization of these response tools to communicate concerns to the faculty. "We write out this concern, this tension in the surveys that come to us" to have courses that "touch more the reality of society." At the time of the interviews, the faculty did not mention the surveys when asked about sources or criteria for evaluating the curriculum.

The seminary's decision to seek civil accreditation opened a door for a non-faith-based public organization to review, advise, and expect compliance with its guidelines. The risks posed by this regulatory oversight were regarded as lesser than the greater anticipated benefits. Seminary A, like other Protestant seminaries, with its foreign and non-Catholic origins, represents a minority population in Spain. Identification with civic accreditation standards signifies a high degree of voluntary contextual engagement with Spanish higher education and, as the survey participants indicated, with a society that values higher education.

In an analysis of Lithuanian business schools' motives for seeking accreditation, Yelena Istileulova and Darja Peljhan discovered that "legitimacy rather than improved performance" was often the underlying aim for pursuing accreditation.[35] Considering the historic Spanish Protestant quest to defend their legitimacy as Spaniards, it is reasonable to conclude that affirmation of legitimacy as a reputable Spanish institution of higher education factored into the seminary's aims. The seminary's commitment to "maintain in essence" what they had at the core of their curriculum indicates a preexisting high level of internal satisfaction with their institutional objectives, further supporting legitimacy over improved performance as a primary goal

---

33. UEBE Facultad de Teología, "Memoria del título," 172–79.
34. UEBE Facultad de Teología, "Memoria del título," 170.
35. Istileulova and Peljhan, "Institutional Change," 292.

in seeking to be recognized as a civilly accredited institution. The pursuit of legitimacy has been a historic theme for Spanish Protestants.

Church Relations

Seminary A's relationship with the Spanish Protestant church is integral to their mission. It is the critical context within which they dialogue, serve, and critique. The interview data highlighted the fragility of the Spanish Protestant church manifested through economic, theological, and social-relational weaknesses. Being both within and outside of the church, the seminary seeks ways to empower and serve the church as well as to stay in step with ongoing developments, such as its changing demographics.

The Seminary's Relationship with the Church

According to Rector A, the seminary offers educational hospitality at their residential campus and sends both faculty and students to minister in local congregations.

> We form the people that churches send us so that they can serve in their churches. Also, we provide elements of reflection. . . . Therefore we facilitate material of analysis. We organize conferences of information that we open to the churches. . . . Additionally, we have the regular program of studies that we offer during the academic year. We do these types of activities opening it to the churches so that pastors and interested people can participate.

He also emphasized that the seminary professors "*always*, if possible, . . . during the time they are here, are pastors" (emphasis original).

Rector A cited the seminary's reach into churches across Spain through the diaspora of its graduates. "There are many needs that we hope that our graduates can complete and they are doing it, through service, through commitment, through fulfilment of their ministries. . . . Our students are the best ambassadors of . . . the faculty of theology." Faculty A–13 focused on connections formed with churches through current students and faculty. "The students do their practices in the church, therefore that also connects us with the actual world, and also all of the professors are, almost all, are pastors in churches. With this we are in the real world." Her phrase "real world" implies the context of the local churches. Based on her statement, the seminary must leave its campus to participate in the real world of the church, perhaps she is suggesting that the church is more in touch with or influenced by the non-confessing society.

Local churches reciprocate by sending their members to study. Student A-6 said, "[My church] . . . considered that I should be better prepared. . . . I have their complete support to be here with the intention of being able to apply [my education] at church." Churches voluntarily participate in the formation of students by entering into formal agreements between the seminary, local pastors, and their church councils to arrange student ministry practice opportunities.[36] Student A-10 spoke with satisfaction about his placement experience. "We have had opportunities to preach, to go out to evangelize, to work with youth. . . . The work that I do with the church is complete."

The church also seeks counsel from the seminary. Rector A noted,

> The churches expect of the faculty of theology that they give answers to the theological questions that are being planted [in relationship to the society] because they are opening different fronts, and the denomination also expects that the faculty provide resources to respond to this and certainly, all of this is a burden of work, every time greater, for an institution with . . . reduced dimensions.

Faculty A-13 independently confirmed Rector A's statement that the church looks to the faculty for assistance, but the provision of that support taxes the energies of the seminary's personnel.

> One of the things that is most requested of us by our churches are resources—resources for . . . the local church. . . . [They request] material, indigenous material and there we have difficulty to create the material precisely because of the resources, not only financial but also human. We do not have people who can dedicate themselves to this.

In his concluding remarks, however, Rector A admitted that in spite of their present level of engagement, the church still perceives the seminary as a distinct entity from itself.

> It can still be noted, the sensation that the seminaries or the faculty of theology is a place reserved for only specific people who are implicated in theological study. We still need to break this

---

36. UEBE Facultad de Teología, "Memoria del título," 195.

> barrier, to get closer to the churches, and that the churches feel that we are part of them.

Although seminary A willingly and sacrificially engages with the church through its programming, provision of resources, and faculty and students, an invisible barrier between the church and the academy inhibits the seminary from fully functioning as an integral formational component of the church. This tension, being both within and outside of the church, was noted in the statements of people from all three seminaries.

The Seminary's Perceptions of the Church

Another theme that all the seminaries repeatedly highlighted were perceived critical weaknesses within the Spanish Protestant church. Rector A stated, "The evangelical work in Spain is still fragile. It is fragile. It has grown numerically, but it is still fragile." The church faces economic challenges. Faculty A-12 said, "Our churches are generally small; therefore, they only look to have a pastor. . . . The great majority of the churches do not have resources to pay or support more than one person." She mentioned that this is particularly problematic for couples who minister together. "When they arrive at a church . . . [the couple] expect more resources to be able to express their work," but two salaries are not offered. The seminary must consider this economic reality as it prepares its students. Student A-7 addressed the implications of insufficient wages. "About the context that many churches are in, disgracefully, they can't maintain a full-time pastor, so the pastor has to be prepared to be a bi-vocational pastor, . . . to be able to have two professions to support his family." Working bi-vocationally is not necessarily detrimental or undesirable, but the limited financial resources of many churches give pastors no other option. This contextual reality, although labor intensive, may have a serendipitous parallel with the congregational survey data's perception that ministry leaders should know how to help the church to develop a contextually situated theology of work. Employment both within and outside the context of the church would give ministry leaders an inside perspective on the labor context of their parishioners and give them another means of practicing relational ministry in the community, also valued by the survey participants.

The interviewees talked about weak or undeveloped theological formation within the churches. Student A-1 discovered this weakness within himself through his studies.

> You become aware [at seminary] that we do not think profoundly much in the churches. . . . We have some prejudices about many [biblical] passages, or about the history of the church, and when you arrive here, they fall. They fall down.

He finished his interview saying,

> I think that the churches from where we come from, many of us, we are not very aware. . . . To educate in a Christian form this society and our churches, we need to come through here [the seminary]. This I have clear. I had it a little bit clear before, but now that I am here, *more*. (Emphasis original.)

Lack of awareness of this vulnerability in the faith community's theological formation, as student A-1 has recognized, may lead to congregational theological naivety and consequently uninformed theological reflection. The church sends and supports students, but this data suggests that it does not prioritize the theological formation of all its members. Farley's question, posed in 1988, remains valid for the church culture depicted in this research: "How is it that the church continues to settle for the premodern pattern of educated clergy and uneducated laity?"[37]

Faculty A-13 used the imagery of rapidly moving distinct streams of water flowing simultaneous within one river to describe the theological threats facing the church. "The things that [are] concerning in the evangelical world where we currently are . . . in the theological level . . . are distinctive currents that are entering very strongly in our churches." She identified one current as "false spiritualities that are entering our churches and . . . instead of dedicating [themselves] to study, [people say], 'I want something rapid. The Holy Spirit inspires me!'" She says, the Spirit does, "but also through formation and the process that this signifies." She expressed concern. "We are living in the moment that . . . theological education in these levels of the formal manner is being discredited . . . and we do not know the damage that we are doing to *ourselves* and to the church [by] discrediting the formation. It is necessary" (emphasis original). She identified a reason for this disregard: "the influence of the world."

> I use; I grab a thing. I use it quickly. Now it does not serve me and I throw it away. . . . There is a disregard of knowledge and knowing. People rise quickly, running without studies, and I believe that this has a certain part of influence.

---

37. Farley, *Fragility of Knowledge*, 85.

The power and uncontrollability of these currents pose threats to a theologically weak church particularly when these currents communicate messages encouraging anti-intellectualism, hyper-spirituality, and instant gratification. Faculty A-13's observations reflect awareness of the current cultural context, and they echo the rector's concern that the church, even though it asks for help and sends students, does not function in partnership with formal theological education. Faculty A-13 described the difficulty of the situation from the seminary's perspective. It is as if "[we are] moving in a terrain, a bit ambiguous, and it is difficult to create equilibrium."

The church may also be ill-equipped to serve the diverse needs of its neighbors. Several students expressed concern about the church's inability to engage with the social and psychological needs of the local community. Student A-9 said,

> A society wounded by itself and by its sin is going to ask for help from the church and what will we do? . . . [People] will arrive at church with severe problems of identity and with wounds as much on their physical as on their psyche. What will we do with that? I have no idea.

Student A-1 noted another area of weakness in the churches' response to immigrants:

> Now . . . with the arrival of refugees and this transcultural world that is invading the churches, they need to know, to have programs of how to take hold of the topic of paperwork, . . . how to help them to get work . . . [and] to connect them with the . . . Spanish culture.

Rector A recognized the necessity of equipping students to serve multicultural congregations, citing the influx of immigrants, but he did not mention if or how the seminary had begun to move towards that goal. He did acknowledge that the church is not reaching the community of Spain, meaning Spaniards, a fact also noted by one of the students. This is, and has been for some years, Spain's ecclesial and social reality; this suggests that the seminary should move quickly from recognition of this reality to implementing formation that equips their students to serve multicultural congregations who may have complex social and psychological needs.

From the seminary's perspective, the Spanish Protestant church is economically poor, theologically fragile, and ill-equipped to serve the needs of its multicultural and often emotionally and socially wounded congregations. Several limitations hinder seminary A's effectiveness to resource and theologically equip the local churches: their own fragility and lack of personnel, a relational-educational barrier between the "real world" of the church and the seminary, and its own hesitancy to make contextually needed adaptations.

Societal Engagement

The Frame of Society

Although the church represents the primary community in which the seminary participates, the society of Spain with its cultural, political, and demographic diversity represents the local context in which the seminary has developed and continues to function. When asked if the Spanish social context presents distinctive contextual challenges for the seminary, Rector A began with a brief description of the political-religious context.

> In this moment we have various fronts [of concern] that are a cause for reflection for us. For one part, the relationship of the church with the society. It is a frame in which we live. The case of Spain is unique because it is an a-confessional state, for one part, but in practice it is confessional. At the same time, the state maintains agreements of cooperation with [non-Catholic entities]. In Spain they are Muslims, Protestants and Jews. Therefore, for one part, we have to channel how to handle this relationship.

The metaphor of a frame implies boundaries; a frame could limit freedoms, provide security, or define identity. It is notable that he places Protestants, which includes the seminary, inside the frame. There is no indication that the frame is negative, but the rector's particular concern is the relationship that Spain's a-confessional state exercises with Muslims, Jews, and Protestants. Although Spain's laws continue to develop along a-confessional lines, he alludes to lingering vestiges of the Roman Catholic Church's political influence or preferential status in relation to other faith confessions. Subtle political-religious discrimination continues to exert a measure of influence requiring that seminary A be circumspect as it negotiates its relationship with society.

Societal developments challenge the seminary to be observant and responsive to the world around them. Rector A stated, "We need to know our social reality." Student A-4 voiced a similar concern.

> [Knowing the social reality is] so necessary because of the crisis that has happened in Spain and the political change too now since all the autonomies have a social presence in all of them.... I think it's necessary to understand the place where we are right now.

As noted by faculty A-13, the seminary struggles to keep pace with societal change: "The world runs too much; it is difficult to adapt to the environment." She continued: "The church goes at total velocity adapting itself to the world and the new technologies; for example, it is a challenge to adapt ourselves to the new technology, that is truthfully really significant." The changes in Spain's society since the 1980s have been rapid and extensive, and at times directly opposed to many traditional doctrines and beliefs of the church. Change occurs slowly within the seminary as evidenced by the limited scope of revisions in their course of study over nearly a hundred years. Scarcity of resources frustrates the realization of many of their plans. This is their contextual reality.

Limited Points of Contact with Society

Some of the faculty function as external points of contact with the society. Faculty A-13 remarked: "Many of our professors are people who are very qualified, they are invited into different areas of education and not only in the evangelical area, but also in the secular." However, student A-1 critiqued the faculty's limited engagement with the local community: "The faculty could be more present before the society. . . . I have made them know to make themselves more visible to the community where we live." Student A-6 mentioned a concern that the faculty were not providing sufficient guidance on how to connect with the surrounding society. "I think we could be more contextualized . . . regarding the Spanish community. . . . Faculty could be more with subjects that are more practical to know society, people, to be closer. . . . I'm missing tools [to be] more in contact with society."

Seminary A describes Spanish society in their accreditation report as: "an advanced society that requires professional answers to its necessities as well as its uncertainties."[38] Student A-10, a South American, has recognized that he must adjust his form of engagement with Spain's advanced society. "One has to adapt; Spain is not bad. The . . . bad perspective is the one I have, to think that Spain has to be the way I want it to be."

---

38. UEBE Facultad de Teología, "Memoria del título," 9.

He has encountered Spanish resistance to conversations about faith. "The Spaniard [is] a bit more critical . . . even if . . . you identify yourself. 'Yes, yes,' they say. [But] they don't want it."

Other students emphasized the contextual necessity of being well-prepared to converse with Spanish society, reflected also in their suggested additional courses. Student A-9 said,

> I think it's indispensable to be able to dialogue with a world that asks for reason. It asks [the] reason [for] our faith and if you don't know what's being investigated, what the big minds are investigating, saying, contradicting, or contributing to what is Bible study or theology in general, well, . . . you're going to be . . . defenseless, . . . an unprepared voice.

Student A-2 agreed, not only about the importance of a well-prepared apologetic argument, but also about the integrity of one's life.

> The people of the world are very well prepared. And we need to prepare ourselves not only to confront this world. . . . Rather, when people prepare themselves, they can give correct answers to the people because the people of this world need answers because they are fed up with religion. . . . And we need to be people that give true answers because the people can see if we are living what we say.

These comments represent a conceptualization of Spanish society as sophisticated, educated, and religiously disinterested in the beliefs of others. The underlying questions are: To what extent is theological education responsible to equip and supply its students with knowledge, experience, formation, and tools for effective engagement with the non-confessing society? And to what extent are the students responsible for their own learning? Attitudes towards and expectations of theological formation are also contextually situated issues that are important to observe and to take into consideration in the design and practices of theological education.

The seminary must find ways to keep up with the world and their local society for the purpose of offering students theological wisdom and good practice. Historic divisions between Protestants and Catholics remain in the memories of the faculty, even though they now find themselves together within the same frame. Seminary A's students recognize the importance of informed dialogue with Spanish society, a formative practice that does not depend on financial resources, but on theological reflection and relational understanding. The seminary's resource-poor state hinders it from taking critical steps towards advancement, particularly in the area of technology, leaving it running behind developments in the society. Civil accreditation, an excellent library, respected faculty, forty-five years in the local community, and socially aware students are significant resources to begin moving towards and regaining ground in their contextualized social engagement.

Seminary A and the Four Continua

Seminary A has historic theological and denominational roots in Spain. They have persevered through Francoist persecution and the continuing vestiges of religious discrimination. The faculty are well educated. Their residential campus is located on the outskirts of Spain's capital, Madrid. They grant civilly accredited bachelor's and master's degrees. Churches send their people to the seminary to study and open their doors to student practitioners. Yet, serious challenges confront the seminary as it seeks to balance its historical design and doctrinal commitments with the need to adapt to ever-changing contextual realities in the church and society of Spain.

Seminary A's alignment on the four continua would be as follows: *For whom is theological education?* Education primarily targets a select minority of ministry-oriented students. *What educational methodology is utilized?* They incorporate both cognitive and experiential formation through student practice placements in local churches, yet the methodology is weighted towards cognitive mastery of content. *What is the aim or purpose?* Ministry development is prioritized over faith development. And *where does the seminary locate itself in relation to church and society?* The seminary is physically external to the churches, yet relationally connected with them, particularly those within its own denomination, even though there is a degree of perceived tension or divide between the academy and the church. Although the seminary is surrounded by the local community, the campus maintains a cloistered ethos.

Figure 3 Seminary A Continua

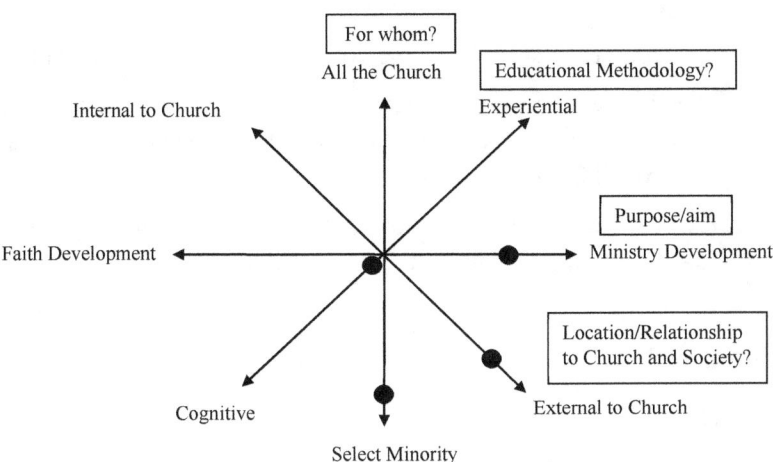

Revision of their current design will require that they determine what is theologically essential to maintain doctrinal integrity and what current design elements and practices can be cast off so that they can gain equilibrium and run along with both the church and the society. Although their resources are limited, their heritage of sacrificial commitment to their students, the institution, and the church may be anchoring factors to sustain them through the ongoing process of contextual adaptation, as it has done for over one hundred years, and most recently through the arduous task of achieving civil accreditation.

Questions for Reflection on the Case Study of Seminary A

1. Keeping in mind the historical contexts of theological education and Spain's Protestants and the perspectives of the survey participants, in what ways is seminary A adapting its designs and practices for the unique context of the church in Spain? Give two or three examples. What is missing or could be improved?

2. Seminary A is committed to its historic mission and to the four focus areas of their curriculum, yet the students are concerned that they will not be prepared to minister to the local community. What kinds of adjustments could be made to the curriculum, the delivery of courses,

or to other aspects of the seminary's design and practices to equip the students in some of the areas that they mentioned without adding more courses? Give two or three suggestions.

3. How can mentorships be incorporated into theological education?
4. What is the role or responsibility of theological institutions when they serve in a context where the churches are theologically weak and prone to fall into "entering currents"?
5. How important is accreditation in your context? What are the costs? How or does it add value to theological education?

Seminary B

The Context

Seminary B has persevered through more than 125 years of diverse challenges, requiring continuous adaptation to the changing context of Spain. From its beginning as a small denominational institution in southern Spain, to its current ecumenical, fully online presence based in Madrid, seminary B has demonstrated its commitment to continue through relocations, restructuring, and the formation of new relationships.

The Historical Context

The seminary was founded in 1884 in Cadiz and is the oldest Protestant seminary in Spain.[39] During the oppressive years of Francoist Spain, the seminary dispersed its operations to various locations across Spain and operated in a "semi-clandestine" manner.[40] Faculty B-3 commented,

> [The seminary] is very old. In fact, it comes from the late nineteenth century. It has [had] changing names and changing places. [It] has been in different parts of Spain. It was closed by the Spanish police in the fifties but it was here in . . . this building [in Madrid]. In the late fifties the police came to . . . close [this place]. . . . The students had to move to Barcelona. . . . [The pastors were] teaching in private houses.

---

39. SEUT Facultad de Teología, "Memoria del título," 12.
40. SEUT Facultad de Teología, "Memoria del título," 9.

Although the seminary experienced frequent relocations over its trajectory, the faculty continued to offer in-person classroom instruction until they made their initial venture into distance learning in the 1990s. Its preference for face-to-face theological formation was an underlying factor in the 2003 relocation to El Escorial, a town forty-five minutes north of Madrid. The property offered ample space for offices, library, dormitory living for single and married students, a chapel, gardens, and accessibility for commuters. However, the number of students remained low. When the 2008 financial crisis devastated Spain's economy, the seminary had to evaluate the viability of its residential program. Simultaneously, it was working towards the newly attainable civil accreditation for Protestant seminaries. In 2012–13 the seminary initiated its fully online degree in theology. Due to the apparent redundancy of the residence facilities and the high cost of maintaining a large physical campus outside the city, the seminary relocated to Madrid in 2016.

The Physical Context

Seminary B's current physical campus is located in an established inner-city neighborhood of Madrid. The oldest city subway line has a stop near the seminary entrance. The building designated for the seminary's use holds recently renovated offices, a faculty communal area, a library with over eighteen thousand holdings, and several multipurpose rooms. Additionally, it has use of the campus chapel located in an adjacent building. Although the faculty teach online, maintaining an institutional physical presence preserves its historic footprint in Spain.

The Relational Context

The spacious, gated, historically Protestant-owned property belongs to the Fliedner Foundation. In 1870, Frederick Fliedner, a German, was sent to Spain as a missionary to encourage the development of Protestantism during the period of religious freedom after the Inquisition.[41] Education is one of the three primary foci of the Fliedner Foundation.[42]

---

41. "Historia de la Fundación," Fundación Federico Fliedner, para. 2.
42. "Quienes somos," Fundación Federico Fliedner, para 1.

Seminary B has historic and continuing affiliations with two of the oldest Protestant denominations in Spain, the Iglesia Evangélica de España (IEE) and the Spanish Reformed Episcopal Church. In 2000, the IEE signed an agreement with the Fliedner Foundation giving it a legal and primary role in the governance of the seminary.[43] The agreement facilitates the seminary's use of the foundation's resources, including properties, promotional venues, secure data storage systems, and informational technology support. Perhaps most significantly, the foundation provides substantial financial support.[44] The foundation has representation, along with the seminary faculty, in the System of Internal Quality Control and a representative on the Quality Commission, which evaluates the faculty and function of the institution.[45] Rector B spoke about the additional responsibility to provide historical and doctrinal orientation to employees of the foundation that this relationship has placed on the seminary.

> It is a foundation that has grown a lot in personnel. Not all of the personnel are believers or evangelical. . . . There are some who are Catholics who would say they are believers. Others who would say they are not practicing. . . . This is a mandate that . . . we would have now that we are in Madrid to . . . prepare some course . . . for the new personnel [of the Fliedner Foundation,] . . . more than 300 persons.

It is important to note that FEREDE has independent legal oversight of the seminary to ensure its compliance with civil accreditation and to advocate for its liberties as a recognized faith-based organization. Seminary B's institutional relationships exhibit its commitment to ecumenical collaboration that prioritizes Christian scholarship and investigation.

---

43. ANECA, "Informe de autoevaluación," 2.

44. In 2018–19, the total amount paid towards expenses of the seminary, including the salaries for five seminary employees was 309,045€. S41 Auditoría y Consultoría, "Informe," Feb. 2020, 45–46. In 2022–23, the total amount, with only three employees, was 177,756€. S41 Auditoría y Consultoría, "Informe," Feb. 2024, 48–49.

45. The SEUT Quality Commission includes the dean, director of studies, the academic committee, a Fliedner representative, an additional professor, a current student, and a member of the seminary support staff. The founding denomination would have representation through faculty associated with it. SEUT Facultad de Teología, "Memoria del título," 105.

The Instructional Context

Although seminary B's faculty offices and library represent its physical presence in Spain, its instructional presence has moved online. The seminary states that provision of online education is an ideal way to offer theological formation to the target student group: "laity with intellectual questions."[46] However, it continues some in-person instruction through theological workshops and seminars offered on the campus, in local churches, and in venues such as Comillas Pontifical University. The seminary values this engagement with the wider Christian faith community as a means of maintaining contextual relevance.[47]

Building on its previous experiences in distance learning, the seminary, with the support of the Fliedner Foundation, has committed to training the faculty in the use of online educational platforms, which were integrated into their course delivery before the pandemic.[48] The transition to online instruction has meant that the faculty have had to surrender their preference for in-person theological education.

Seminary B's online classes are small, typically five or six students. Rector B said that the smaller class size facilitates both the transfer of "theoretical content" and the development of "personal knowledge. . . . [The students] have trust to say things, . . . [to] reveal themselves." Faculty B-1 spoke of her efforts to investigate a process for transitioning the current format of asynchronous interactive forums to a higher level of synchronous inter-activity. "Now [it] is difficult to find a time [to meet in real time] because of people's schedules, . . . but we need to get to a place where [synchronous] interview online produced once a week would be more natural between the student and the professors."

Mission and Identity

Academics and Faith

Seminary B's mission is to be an institution "where faith and rigorous study are united to offer theological formation adapted for the challenges in the

---

46. SEUT Facultad de Teología, "Memoria del título," 12–13.
47. ANECA, "Informe de autoevaluación," 14.
48. SEUT Facultad de Teología, "Memoria del título," 77–78.

culture, society, and the church in which we live."⁴⁹ The academic emphasis of the Berlin model on theological education is firmly embedded into its mission and identity. Yet, it is counter balanced with a measure of the Athens model and its classical emphasis on *paideia*, represented in their dedication to facilitate the faith development of their students.

Unlike seminary A, which prioritizes equipping people for vocational ministry, the faculty of seminary B highlighted their commitment to academic formation in theology. Faculty B-1 noted,

> These are serious studies, university level, and for this it requires consistence, rigor, capacity, and above all else to be present and to understand what it is to be in a university environment even though it is in an ecclesial environment.

The academic and professional qualifications of the faculty corroborate their prioritization of scholarly excellence. Considering the minority status of the Protestant population in Spain and the typical number of registered students, ranging between twenty-three to forty-one per semester from 2012 to 2021, the concentration of gathered academic expertise is significant.⁵⁰

Although seminary B has students who study to fulfil a vocational call, the faculty repeatedly stressed that the seminary primarily serves anyone seriously interested in studying theology. Ecumenism is the overarching context that broadens the reach of their theological horizons and openness to a diverse student population. Faculty B-1 said,

> Our model student is not usually a person that looks for a specific pastoral formation, but studies because of a curiosity, studies because one is now a pastor and wants to [be] continu[ally] equipping and forming oneself, studies because one wants to collaborate in one's community, but it is not . . . because of one's vocational call.

The seminary's academic rigor is balanced by its parallel commitment to nurture faith through the pastoral care of students. Faculty B-2 said, "Our vision, certainly, is that the academic formation, that it be good, that it be solid, without forgetting . . . [to attend to the] more pastoral side [of formation]." Faculty B-1 explained, "Therefore we try to give much attention . . . that there is growth of faith . . . . and in addition to our focusing

---

49. "Bienvenido del decano," para 1.
50. SEUT Facultad de Teología, "Informe de la Facultad," 4.

on more spiritual companionship. . . . [Yet,] what greatly characterizes the faculty is the academic rigor."

The Course of Study

To fulfil their mission, the seminary offers a government accredited undergraduate degree in theology, a nonaccredited version of that degree for those who do not meet the accreditation admission requirements or who intentionally choose that option, and a nonaccredited diploma in theology that follows the same plan of study as the undergraduate degree minus biblical languages. The curriculum covers four primary areas: Bible and biblical Languages, theology and church history, pastoral theology, and investigation (including research methods), which includes ten credits for a final research project chosen by the student and approved by the faculty. This is a summative, integrative project; discovery of new knowledge is not required.[51] The structure of their course of study implements a variation of the fourfold model.[52] They have combined theology and church history into one area of concentration, which allows them to include individual investigation as the fourth element, yet the classic fourfold subject areas remain at the core of the curricular design.

Identity

Each interviewee affirmed the scholarly qualifications of the seminary's faculty and level of instruction. Faculty B-4 stated, "We form a group of professors very well equipped." Faculty B-5 estimated that "the quality as far as the academic level is probably a bit higher than some of the other schools [in Spain]. . . . [The seminary] has tremendous potential as far as their academic level." This was another thread in the theme of legitimacy's importance.

The interviews highlighted three defining factors in seminary B's identity: ecumenism, inclusivity, and scarcity. Ecumenism is an intrinsic and historic component of its identity. It influences and supports their intellectual openness as well as with whom they choose to collaborate, including the Roman Catholic Church, a historically sensitive issue in Spain.

---

51. SEUT Facultad de Teología, "Trabajo fin de bachillerato," 6.
52. Farley, *Theologia*, 23.

Its founding denomination, IEE, embraced ecumenism when the World Council of Churches was formed in 1948. Rector B substantiated the reasoning for this position.

> [The seminary] had to be ecumenical and also . . . very dialogical, . . . less centered in theological alignments [and] more centered in the academic quality . . . that would permit us to have professors that would be more conservative [and others who are] more open, more liberal, but that they would have the capacity of dialogue.

Ecumenism is integral for understanding their distinctive mission within Spain. Faculty B-2 stated because faculty have "open[ed] themselves to other methods of study that, according to [some], are more liberal, . . . we believe we are necessary." According to Rector B, this is one of their distinctive features: "We have a line of relatively open thinking. . . . I do not think we are liberal, but in the world of the Spanish [Protestant] environment, well, [it is] as if we were."

Generally, Spanish Protestant evangelical communities tend to be theologically conservative.[53] Faculty B-2 spoke of the repercussions of the seminary's ecumenical practices.

> There are churches that do not want to know anything about us because they think that we use methods that are not biblical, that we study things that are not necessary for the faith because [for those churches] . . . only the Bible is necessary.

In her closing statements, she expressed her hope, despite her perceptions of the evangelical community's opinion about the seminary. "I would like that . . . many people would [be] freer to be able to come and study with us. . . . Today they don't feel free . . . because they . . . say, "No, no, no, this cannot be because it is almost sin." (Drops her voice.) "It is almost sin." (Brings it back to a normal volume. Speaks slowly and deliberately). "It is almost sin." Faculty B-1 echoed a similar perception with a graphic metaphor. "There are people who believe that the labor of this faculty is not labor, [that] it is the contrary, that it is practically the herald of Armageddon."

Their theological liberalism is not the only issue with which other Protestants take issue. Faculty B-3 noted, "[It] is the only [Protestant seminary] that has an interest in a more ecumenical openness especially to Catholics." Consequently, he continued, "[It]'s a problem for us to connect with the evangelical public in Spain." Nevertheless, they do not allow

---

53. ANECA, "Informe de autoevaluación," 1.

these negative narratives to alter their identity nor hinder their mission. Faculty B-2 explained,

> We help ... people [to] have more critical thinking than what [the more conservative communities] are placing before them.... You have to study ... because you have to also give an answer to people ... on the street ... who do not confess to be believers.... We are not saying, "You have to believe this." We are saying, "Notice what there is.... Now, you discern. How do you see this? How do you see the other? Dialogue with us." And we give [students] some guidelines and tools ... so that [they] can be autonomous, so they don't have to sing like a parrot [to] whatever [their] pastor says. ... Therefore, yes, we have stories of people who have felt liberated from a yoke.

Seminary B regards itself as a countermeasure to fundamentalist teaching, and it provides a context where students can experience theological liberation. For these practices, it is marginalized by the wider Protestant evangelical community yet remains unwavering in its commitment to ecumenism and the theology that supports it. Rector B stated, "We are not going to reach great multitudes because our form of thinking is not attractive to the great mass.... We are not going to offer them what they ask."

The seminary's ecumenism is practiced through inclusivity, an openness to those from diverse backgrounds and contexts. Faculty B-3 noted, "We are open to everyone.... We don't have a restriction. We don't have like a faith statement that you have to sign to be a student." Two faculty members illustrated this practice of inclusivity by sharing stories of their experiences as students in the seminary. Faculty B-4 shared,

> The professors welcomed me.... I came from a context much more fundamentalist, and the truth is that they had a great amount of patience with me, much understanding. This made me see that they were people who paid attention to the integral formation of the student. This truthfully encouraged me, and I said, I wanted to continue collaborating with this institution.... I went little by little realizing, at the hand of my professors, of the necessity that I had to amplify my mind, my knowledge.

Faculty B-3 said,

> When I found [seminary B] I found a place where people were happy to hear what I was saying, even if at times I think they were not understanding what I was talking about because it was a

completely different thing.... And through these twenty years, we have developed all this area [of science and faith].... I think because of the situation of the evangelical church in Spain, I couldn't have done that probably in any other institution. I think that at [seminary B] they were more willing to take risks in discussing these topics, and in other places I think they were probably very afraid to get into these areas of debate.

Seminary B's aim is to accompany students on a journey of discovery and to equip them with tools to reflect, investigate, and discern truth. Faculty B-3 explained,

Because some of the students come from this kind of [fundamental] background, when they arrive and study theology.... they discover things they didn't know.... "Why didn't anyone [tell] me about these things?"... Some people can react having some fear and they could abandon studies.... So, something that we would like... to do in the future is to have more pastoral care for these kinds of situations,... [to] help them to see that there is a way to be a Christian in spite of all those things that you learn that seem to be challenges.... The solution is not to just jump from sanity and abandon everything.

Finally, their inclusivity extends to people outside the Protestant community who may represent seminary B's future. Rector B commented,

This is giving us a special satisfaction, the fact that some of these people are examples... [coming] from a place, an environment [of] indifferen[ce], as could be the European in general, or the Spaniard in particular. But if you do a good work... to offer a formation that for whatever reason they consider it attractive, the truth is that... you are doing a good job with these people. And there will be more, I think, this type of people who come from an environment that is irreligious, from the "edges."... And now, yes, this indicates to us that perhaps we need to busy ourselves,... when we work on the contents, in this type of profile, in this type of people. We can offer there something important.

These examples of inclusivity offered to three students—a fundamentalist, a scientist, and a non-religious person—support the seminary's practice of wide-ranging inclusivity even though it may contribute to their marginalization in the wider Protestant community.

The seminary's identity is also shaped by comprehensive scarcity. First on the list of challenges noted by Rector B was "economic survival; it is very difficult to survive in the Spanish context." Faculty B-1 said, "[Financial need] is a challenge that I believe, that we will never lose. It is a reality, ours, that one lives in Spain, in Spanish Protestantism, and one needs to know how to make the best of it, no? And live in its best consequences, trying to bring out the best game." It is financially dependent on the Fliedner Foundation, which, although it is a generous organization, has its limitations as faculty B-1 noted. "[The Foundation] supports much the solvency of the institution . . . and at times they do not have all of the economic resources that we would like but even so the faculty continues."

Its financial dependence on one foundation places seminary B in a precarious position. The website invites people to join "circles of friends" to financially support students and to purchase resources such as books, writing that it "conduct[s] many of their activities without charge, and others barely covering a part of the actual cost."[54] Generosity and endowments only partially represent reasons for the practice of providing inexpensive formation. The assumptions of some people in the churches are also a factor. Faculty B-2 explained.

> Many people feel [seminary tuition] to be expensive because they do not know all the work that is behind the scenes. . . . Sometimes the people think . . . we should give it freely since we are working for God. Therefore, they believe that they have the right to study without paying.

They also struggle with low enrollment numbers and low student retention rates in the online platform that negatively impact their ability to function. Faculty B-3 noted,

> There's a declining number of students as the year progresses . . . because not everyone really wants to, other times because they don't really have time, ... [and] most of them because it is online. They study only a few subjects. . . . They do [it] from home; they have jobs [and] families so . . . they find that the studies [are] more complicated.

Scarcity is a constant threat. Faculty B-2 said, "We are going to end up almost not being able to do our work because there is no money. There is no money. There is no money." Her voice became quieter with each repetition. Faculty B-1 voiced the same ominous possibility of closure, yet she highlighted the positive lessons learned from scarcity.

54. "Círculo de amigos," lines 5–6.

> Clearly things cost us much more [in every way, not only financially], but I believe that this has given us a certain character, a certain way of doing things, to not always privilege the urgent.... Institutions like ours, that are always at their limit, the year that is coming we don't know if we will still be here [laughter]. Well, this could be good because it gives you the capacity to optimize the resources ... But it can also be very tiring.

Despite the challenges of limited resources and perceived marginalization from many in Spain's Protestant community, seminary B maintains its mission to offer scholarly theological education and to facilitate the faith development of its diverse student body. Its identity and mission of theological openness and inclusivity offer a pathway to explore theology in a context of ecumenical freedom. However, inclusivity has not significantly increased their enrollment numbers.

The Contextualization of the Curriculum

The Curriculum's Historical Foundations

Seminary B's curriculum has its foundational roots in the Open Theological College (OTC), founded "in the early 1990s as a partnership of six UK Bible Colleges" to provide an accredited distance-learning theology degree.[55] It is the source, according to faculty B-1, of the seminary's "inherited ... English perspective." Prior to OTC, they looked to South America for validated programs, but Rector B noted: "We began using this material [from the biblical Latin American seminary] but we saw that it did not fit because it was a ... very distinct material, as much pedagogically as well as ideologically; it came from another very distinct context; it didn't fit." The seminary reports that it chose to sign an agreement with OTC in 1997 because it was a European program, compatible with Spanish Protestantism, validated, academically excellent, balanced with practical pastoral application, ecumenical, and because it encouraged critical inquiry.[56] An unforeseen benefit was that it also set them in good standing to move towards compliance with the European Bologna System.

The decision to adopt English language course materials committed the seminary to a labor-intensive translation task. According to faculty B-1

---

55. Pitkanen, "Hermits," 150.
56. SEUT Facultad de Teología, "Memoria del título," 15–17.

this facilitated the "contextualization of the materials . . . to the Spanish reality." The translation process required the Spanish faculty to filter the course materials through their own contextual and cultural frameworks. Like seminary A, indigenous faculty were critical in the contextualization of the course materials, however no details for how they undertook that process were mentioned.

OTC was later incorporated into Gloucester University, Cheltenham, in 2002, and the decision was made to revise the course of study. Rather than transition with OTC and commit to the translation of new materials, seminary B requested and received the proprietary rights to the original OTC plan of studies. Rector B said,

> We followed our own [way] but we inherited a little of the logic that had been in these materials, the structure [and] content we inherited. Later we went changing little by little, but very little by little, . . . adapting it every . . . so often to the Spanish context. But no, we have [not] made . . . great big changes, except [in] a few subjects and we have made a few new [subjects].

Part of the logic that they inherited was OTC's practice of studying theology and church history as one integral focus. Faculty B-1 explained.

> This traditionally in Spain has not been like this, they always separated . . . the history of the church and the history of theology, but . . . we [understand] that the context also explains the "whys" and the "hows" therefore we have not separated one discipline from the other.

Their current plan of studies was developed through consultation with the academic committee, cabinet of professors, and a student representative. It was reviewed externally by FEREDE, the other civilly accredited Spanish Protestant seminaries, and a representative from the IEE also had input on behalf of the denomination.[57]

Contextualization's Impact on the Means of Delivery

Their transition to the online delivery represents their most recent contextualization challenges. Faculty B-1 said,

---

57. SEUT Facultad de Teología, "Memoria del título," 17–18.

> [We have] prepared the [online] pedagogy and didactic reality [of the course materials] so that the students could have the flexibility to study when they wanted to but within certain parameters and within an understanding that permitted them to be coherent, to have a general vision of what is the theological "task."

The contexts of students, rather than churches, were named as key factors driving its decisions to adapt to a different mode of delivery. The versatility of the online platform extends the educational footprint. Faculty B-3 explained.

> We find that the online system gives more flexibility to reach more students that also can be living everywhere in Spain or outside of Spain. It also makes it easier for some of [the] lecturers to work with us because we have people lecturing here that are living in other cities, outside of Spain as well.

The contextualization of this modality requires ongoing innovation technologically and pedagogically. Rector B noted, "[Now] that we are a program online, all the part[s], audio [and] visual, we need to improve . . . to bring ourselves up to date." Faculty B-1 confirmed their commitment to develop their expertise in this new medium.

> We know where we want to go, and now what we lack is to launch out more profoundly into the use of the new didactic technologies. . . . But one has to continue, of course, exploring and pushing above all the didactic line.

The move to online instruction has impacted several of their previous forms of direct involvement with students. In a 2017 self-study, the seminary submitted a proposal to remove the optional supervised ministry practice from the course of study because no students had enrolled in that course. The report noted that many students were already serving in local churches or that ministry was not many students' primary objective.[58] The loss of supervised practical ministry in the curricular design shifts the balance of course work towards the academic study of theology.

The transition to online instruction presented an additional challenge: how to provide pastoral care for students. Rector B noted with concern, "Now that we . . . do not have the [in-person] program, the challenge is greater, . . . especially the pastoral part . . . that requires some type of practices or some type of personal follow-up. How do we do this for the

---

58. ANECA, "Informe de autoevaluación," 19.

student?" They are considering the development of a form of chaplaincy to provide spiritual and emotional support for the students. The online program digitally extends the reach of their theological formation, yet it also restricts its direct and personal involvement in applied forms of student ministry practice.

Accreditation

Civil accreditation allows seminary B to formally identify itself as part of Spain's higher education system. Accreditation opens opportunities for graduates and faculty to connect with other institutions as the seminary aligns itself with Spain's and Europe's standardized norms. Seminary B sought out this form of validation even before it was an official option for Spanish Protestant seminaries. Its commitment to attain and maintain this status is demonstrated through the sacrificial changes it has made, through what faculty B-1 described as the "exponential" effort required to achieve accreditation.

When seminary B entered into the 1997 agreement with OTC, the correspondence format of OTC's program, although important, was a secondary reason for the formation of the partnership. The faculty in Spain was capable of creating its own proficient academic program. OTC offered something that was otherwise unavailable to Spanish Protestant seminaries at that time, official accreditation. Protestants seeking to offer accredited degrees to facilitate entrance into post-graduate studies had no other option but to form agreements with institutions outside Spain.

In 2011, seminary B, like seminary A, became one of five Protestant seminaries to receive Spanish civil accreditation. Faculty B-1 described the tremendous volume of work to meet accreditation requirements.

> This faculty, along with other Spanish Protestant faculties, have received the recognition of [our] studies, but this has obligated us to put ourselves in a system that asks all the universities to complete the same criteria. It is equal whether you have four hundred professors or if you have five. . . . The quantity of processes and systems of quality that we have had to generate has been for us exponentially atmospheric.

Even within the more formalized structure, the faculty have liberty to select their course content. Faculty B-3 said,

> One thing is the content of the subjects, you can change the book or the readings, things like that, but some of the structure of the number of credits and the name, even the name of the subject itself, all these things are regulated now by the government, by this body.... But then inside this ... each lecturer has freedom to update the things they teach.

The freedom to choose content was also highlighted by seminary A.

Faculty B-1 spoke about the historical and political significance of this right to pursue civil accreditation.

> On one hand it has been very good because it was time historically in this country. Finally there was recognition of the civil effects of the Protestants. This has been a step forward, stupendous and great, and it needs to be noted and acknowledged; it is an historic event but also it implies a burden of work that perhaps initially no one had anticipated.

She spoke positively about the impact of the new levels of accountability and transparency.

> Now that we respond to a third [party] we cannot do certain things ... [that] we would do among ourselves [before].... We have to respond to another institution that audits you regularly. ... This obligates us to work in a more professional manner, more rigorous, according to norms, with a transparency that perhaps we did not have before—not because we didn't want it, but because it wasn't necessary.

Rector B noted the new level of accountability with reference to collecting feedback. "When [the accrediting agency] come to do an inspection of quality, they obligate us a bit to enforce doing more surveys and more analyzes of the surveys." He admitted that it is a struggle to collect this data.

> The surveys that the students do are not always complete, because they don't always respond. Therefore, as always, this is the problem. Well, but the advantage is ... that we don't have a great number of students—forty—and the follow up we can do with them is very personal.... In the beginning of each year, [I] have an interview with all of the new entering students. Therefore ... I know them. We see a little of what they aspire to.... All of us [the faculty] know quite well the students that we have. This gives a certain trust to ... speak [with them about] ... what is more useful, where are the problems in the contents or in the foci.

The value placed on information collected through direct dialogue highlights the contextually generated tension within seminary B between online and in-person instruction and the obligation to work according to the norms of accreditation standards versus relational in-house interactions.

Seminary B's compliance with ANECA publicly validates the academic and professional level of the theological education that it is offering.[59] Compliance with Spain's tertiary norms and standards demonstrates educational and organizational contextualization. Yet, there is underlying tension as it tries to maintain the practice of interpersonal communication, preferring direct feedback rather than surveys. Like seminary A, control of course content critically anchors seminary B to its mission and identity.

Church Relations

The seminary states that the needs of the church and society factor into its contextual aims for formational outcomes: "In the actual Spanish context, the object of the degree in Theology is that both ordained ministers and laity attain sufficient training to confront the challenges [facing] the evangelical church and the Spanish society."[60] Although the seminary does not require the faculty to hold pastoral or ministry positions, many do serve in various ministries at local churches. Rector B mentioned a proposal that he had made to try and clarify the relationship of the faculty with the church: ordination of the faculty as theological educators. He said "ordination would help to make [one] conscious [that one] is working for the church, . . . not only for the academic intellectual world."

---

59. FEREDE, the legal advocate for Protestants, monitors compliance with civic accreditation regulations and educational quality. They have a line of communication with the faculty, and with the dean in particular. As part of the relational management, the Fliedner Foundation gives oversight to the System of Internal Guarantee of Quality (SGIC). As an institution with a small number of faculty, staff, and students, the academic committee and the dean are charged with carrying out the procedures of the SGIC, but they include input from faculty, staff, and students. SEUT Facultad de Teología, "Memoria del título," 104–8.

60. SEUT Facultad de Teología "Memoria del título," 11.

The Founding Denomination

With a nationwide membership of 2500, seminary B describes the IEE as a "minority among the minority" of Spanish Protestants.[61] Faculty B-1 described the denomination as "the womb [or origin] of this faculty." However, she continued, "It is also true . . . that the majority of the students do not belong to the IEE. . . . The theology that [the IEE churches] offer attracts certain people, but later the ecclesial practice . . . is not the best in the world." For the seminary, the IEE's small membership reduces the pool of candidates and severely limits options for ministerial placements for graduates. The seminary's 2021 report indicated that there were only five students associated with the IEE.[62]

Although the denomination may historically be the "womb of the faculty," seminary B's relationship with the denomination is not particularly strong. Faculty B-1 said,

> There is not an especially fluid relation between the local communities that form part of the IEE presbytery of Madrid and the faculty. . . . The relationship is articulated more through personal channels rather than institutional, at the local level. At the national level it is a different story, because there is greater fluidity. The channels are more defined. . . . I believe that the relation between the IEE . . . at the local level and the faculty would be good if they would work on it more. . . . It is somewhat disconnected.

This is a critical observation; the IEE churches with the greatest physical proximity to the seminary are the least invested. The reasons for the disconnection were not given. Seminary B's relationship with its affiliated denomination has a completely different character than seminary A's relationship with its affiliated denomination. Seminary A works closely with its denomination and sends students to ministry placements in local churches.

Challenges Facing the Spanish Protestant Church

When asked to list the seminary's challenges, Rector B began with the "fragmented" state of Spain's evangelical church represented in the reluctance of various denominations to collaborate or share resources with one another. Faculty B-1 characterized the divisive attitudes underlying

61. ANECA, "Informe de autoevaluación," 1–2.
62. SEUT Facultad de Teología, "Informe de la facultad," 5.

that fragmentation by contrasting the seminary with the evangelical community. "For me the faculty of [seminary B] supports a seriousness, an elegance, . . . a way of being, a serenity that I believe that we greatly lack in the evangelical Spanish perspective, and [one] can fall very easily into labelling, very easily in conflict."

As faculty B-3 observed, the basis for Protestants' lack of trust of one another may have deep roots in their history of religious persecution.

> This is still very dependent on all the history of persecution that the evangelicals have in Spain, and because of that, which came until the 70s, very recently, people still have a lot of distrust of the Catholic context. It's still not so easy to have this kind of dialogue or even collaboration. . . . But this is something that is still not part of the common background of the Spanish evangelicals. It is not seen with good eyes here.

This statement further clarifies the reasons for the wider evangelical Protestant community's withdrawal from seminary B's ecumenical openness to working with Catholics; the wounds of the past are neither healed nor forgotten. One study by Drelichman et al. reports that lack of trust is one of the characteristics of the communities that experienced inquisitorial persecution.[63]

A perceived lack of theological formation within Protestant churches adds to the complexity of fragmentation. Faculty B-4 commented, "In being this minority, well many years have passed, the people who have attended [Protestant] churches have not been well formed, not only theologically but also at a general cultural level." He further described the impact of this reality.

> The problem is, in our evangelical Spanish context, . . . there is no tradition of theological formation in our churches. Beginning with those who give direction, the leaders, they have thought, actually, that what the people need are things more devotional, things more of the Christian life, but not to go deeper into what they believe and above all in the area of theology.

Raising the levels of the church's theological formation has become even more critical as access to education has expanded and become prioritized across Spanish society. Faculty B-4 noted,

---

63. Drelichman et al., "Long-Run Effects," 1.

> The generations of youth are forming themselves more. . . . They have questions, they have doubts, and many times what the church offers them falls short. . . . There is a necessity in the churches to be able to respond to their doubts at every level, not only theologically, but also daily life, family. I see a great deal of necessity [for] the education of children.

This suggests an additional aspect of the generational differences noted by Rector A: a generational fragmentation set, in this example, in the context of the local church, and its critical responsibility to theologically educate its people.

Faculty B-3 used metaphors of conflict to characterize the challenge of convincing congregants of the value of academic theological education. "When they see . . . theological studies with a kind of more formal academic degree, . . . they get surprised, and they think, 'This is . . . too much' or 'too complicated.' . . . And that's something that we have to fight with." He noted that the discussion of scientific topics was particularly troubling to many Protestants. "We have . . . a lot of war on these discussion of topics . . . like evolution. This is something that is still very problematic for evangelicals in Spain." The seminary's theological workshops and center for science and faith represent its attempts to address this formational gap, "to do good theology . . . [so that] something more disseminated [might] arrive . . . to the pews of the church."

Faculty B-1 listed three factors that she believed were contributing to the church's weakened theological understanding. The first was those who have immigrated to Spain with differing theological backgrounds who have introduced their beliefs and practices into the churches. Secondly, she cited social media and its ability to spread messages in "a more incendiary manner." Thirdly, she described "a mentality . . . that [says,] 'if you don't think like me, you are not a Christian.'" The first two factors represent external influences that have come into the churches, perhaps some of the "entering currents" previously mentioned by seminary A's faculty member. The third factor, a judgmental resistant posture, may be an historically conditioned mindset within Spain's Protestant population.

Of particular concern to the faculty is the scrutiny that some of its students have experienced upon returning to their home churches. Rector B noted,

> In general [the students] are people committed to their churches and . . . later depending on what churches they attend, [those

churches] create a sort of suspicion towards them, because there is an anti-intellectualism very strong. Therefore we have encountered that some have suffered some from this.

This situation and its implications for the practical formation of students is certainly exacerbated by the seminary's decision to curtail the practice of ministry placements, its recognized need to develop online spiritual formation, and its marginalized relationship with the wider evangelical community. Rector B summarized the difficulty of addressing these challenges.

> There is in our opinion . . . a wave of tremendous fundamentalism, . . . and on the other side a charismaticism also over the top. . . . Therefore, yes it concerns us what theology to do in this context, to be able to put some type of criteria . . . of sanity in the middle of this appearance of stirring waters.

Like seminary A, seminary B sees itself in the midst of unpredictable currents that impact its ability to adapt and to respond to the needs of both the church and society. Its relationship with Spain's evangelical community is fragmented primarily due to its more liberal theological position. Yet, it maintains its ecumenical posture even though it hinders the seminary's ability to share its theological resources with Spain's Protestant churches.

The faculty are also concerned for the legacy of Spain's Protestant evangelical community based on its apparent inability to proclaim the reason for its faith with authenticity and informed relevance. Rector B said,

> What type of thinking . . . are [the Spanish evangelical churches] going to inherit? . . . This anti-intellectualism that is there, and that includes . . . that they don't study the Bible as they did before. [It] makes . . . the churches in general maintain a discourse that is forty years old about any topic. . . . They are saying nothing to the society. It is a bit like . . . the Catholic bishops here in Spain. Those Catholic bishops, many of them still think that they are in the time of Franco when they had voice in everything and votes in everything and think that [they] can [still] pontificate.

Rector B's statement can be likened to a prophetic call to the church to wake up. In the context of seminary B's self-confessed strained relationship with the evangelical community, the authority and value of their critique may not be well received by those for whom it is intended.

Societal Engagement

The seminary functions within Spain's society. Overall, the majority of the curriculum follows the traditional track of academic biblical, historical, and applied pastoral theology. It does offer several courses in counseling, and for those seeking to reflect on sociological issues, there are optional elective courses through their agreement with El Instituto Superior de Ciencias Religiosas de Barcelona (ISCREB). The seminary also publicly offers non-accredited theological workshops, a virtual classroom, and seminars led by their center for science and faith. These represent their attempts to make an educational footprint in the society.[64]

The Non-Confessing Society

When speaking about Spanish society, they referenced the general, non-Protestant faith climate of Spain. Faculty B-4 noted Spain's spiritual need and some negative developments in the society's receptivity to the Christian message.

> From a theological point of view, Spain is still a country of mission [laughter]. Sometimes we think of mission as, well, going to countries that are not developed, [that] don't know anything of the gospel. But Spain is also [a] country of mission. . . . Even though this has been traditionally a Catholic country, I believe that a majority percentage has gone to the other extreme. It is a country very, very anti-religious. It claims to be a very atheistic country. We have gone from one extreme to the other, like pendulums.

These comments challenge the notion or stereotype that Spain remains a predominantly Roman Catholic country.

Although the pendulum may have swung from Catholicism to the anti-religious side, the seminary has witnessed signs of spiritual inquisitiveness. Rector B commented, "But something . . . capturing our attention as well is that some people come from an unbelieving environment, . . . and for whatever reasons they are developing a restlessness for theology." The seminary finds itself well-positioned to respond to this restlessness. The faculty are taking this new student profile into consideration in their evaluations and revisions of the curriculum. However, Rector B expressed concern that conservative Protestants might not be as welcoming to this group.

64. SEUT Facultad de Teología, "Informe de la facultad," 7–12.

> With the problems that the actual society has, it is not sufficient [for Protestants] to say no to all of them. It is not sufficient to say, "No, no, no, no," and that's it. One has to approach [people in the society], theologically approach them, pastorally one has to approach them.

This final comment is less a commentary on the society than on the church. It highlights Protestant traits of defensiveness developed through years of religious oppression.

The Roman Catholic Society

Seminary B collaborates with the pontifical seminary in the community of Madrid. Even with the society's growing anti-religiosity, some Roman Catholics are enrolling in the seminary's courses. Faculty B-3 said,

> We have even seen in the last years some students are coming from the Catholic background. . . . They study with us because they want to see how we think. So, this is a new development that is very interesting, very curious. It's also, probably, driven by the situation of the country. You couldn't imagine that fifty years ago, of course, but I think that now we are in that situation where in Spain, people [are] more open to have these things.

This statement sets a counterbalance to the generalization of the swing of the societal pendulum towards religious apathy. Rather than reject faith, some Catholics are pursuing other options such as Protestantism. Seminary B's ecumenism facilitates their receptivity to Catholics.

One people group that was significantly missing in the interview data, either as a representative demographic of the church or of the society, were immigrants. They were only mentioned by one faculty member for bringing different theologies into the Protestant churches. Although seminary B's accreditation document mentions the role that theological formation could play in the enculturation of, specifically, Latin American immigrants into Spain, there were no statements that referred to the realization of that aim.[65] Considering that the percentage of Latin Americans is often the majority in Madrid's Protestant churches, and that there are individuals of Latin American origin in the faculty, this was a curious omission.

---

65. SEUT Facultad de Teología, "Memoria del título," 13.

The Spanish society has swung to a position of general disinterest and even of resistance to Christian faith. Yet there are promising signs evidenced in the spiritual restlessness of several non-confessing students and Catholic inquirers who have approached seminary B seeking theological formation. Shifting its focus to these students may decrease its historical focus on ministerial formation. Seminary B faces choices that may alter its identity, mission, economic survival, and further impact its relationship with the evangelical community of Spain.

Seminary B and the Four Continua

Seminary B's position as the oldest Protestant seminary in Spain testifies to its tenacity. Survival has required multiple relocations and reconfigurations of its design. In addition to acquiring civil accreditation, the most recent adaptation to a fully online instructional platform exhibits its commitment to respond—and perhaps pragmatism in responding—to the contextual realities of Spain and its people. The professionalism of the faculty and their commitment to theological scholarship inspire seminary B's collaboration with Christian academics, both Protestant and Catholic, in a broad range of disciplines. The seminary's historic denominational affiliation with the IEE shapes their ecumenical identity, yet together they have become a minority within a minority.

Seminary B's alignment on the four continua would be as follows: *For whom is theological education?* It is open to all the church and to the wider society, but specifically to those seeking academic formation in theology. Accreditation requirements determine who is qualified to enroll. *Which educational methodology is utilized?* It prioritizes cognitive formation, although it recognizes the need to provide pastoral formational care through chaplaincy. *What is the aim or purpose of theological education?* Academic and faith development are prioritized over ministry development. And *where does the seminary locate itself in relation to the church and to the society?* The seminary is physically external to the church yet geographically centralized in relation to many churches. Its presence is primarily online, electronically accessible to all. Through the practice of ecumenism, it develops partnerships and has significant contact with the local society.

Figure 4 Seminary B Continua

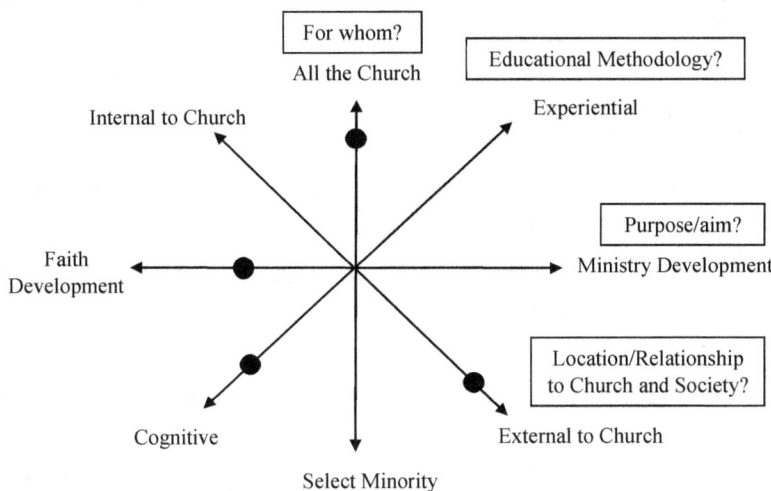

Seminary B faces several critical challenges. Scarcity is their norm. Their dependence on the patronage of the Fliedner Foundation places them in a somewhat precarious situation. The foundation provides many educational resources, but the seminary finds itself in a position of economic vulnerability. Its founding denomination supplies few students and limited options for student ministry placements. Its design and practices have been adapted as its emphasis on scholarship has increased and practical ministry experience has decreased. This transition highlights another loss that the faculty feel deeply in the virtual learning environment: decreased personal face-to-face interaction with students. But perhaps the most serious challenge, based on these interviews, is their marginalization from the greater Protestant evangelical community. It is engaging with some Catholics and a small number of non-confessing students, but the primary sources for theological students and potential ecclesial leaders—the greater evangelical community—stand at a distance. They are wary of seminary B's perceived liberal practices. Finding a way to bridge that gap while simultaneously preserving its ecumenical identity could be life-sustaining, opening a channel for the sharing of wisdom and needed resources.

Questions for Reflection on the Case Study of Seminary B

1. Keeping in mind the historical contexts of theological education and Spain's Protestants, as well as the perspectives of the survey participants, name three ways that seminary B is adapting its designs and practices for the unique context of the church in Spain? What is missing or could be improved?
2. What adaptations would an ecumenical seminary need to make to serve in your context? Give two or three suggestions.
3. In your context, what options are available to theologically curious inquirers or those from other faiths to participate in evangelical theological formation?
4. What are the positives and negatives of online theological education? Give two or three examples. What contextual adjustments would have to be made in your context to faithfully equip ministry leaders or church leaders through online formation?
5. What is the situation of the Protestant evangelical church in your context? Can it function freely or are there restrictions imposed on it? How does your freedom or the lack of it impact the design and practices of your institution or church?

Seminary C

The Context

The Historical Context

Seminary C was established in 2011. It is the youngest and least formalized seminary represented in this book. Seminary C's leadership consulted with Mennonite pastors in Spain and other European countries for over two years to prepare for the inauguration of the institution.[66] The Spanish Anabaptist, Mennonite, and Brethren in Christ Church Association (AMyHCE) commissioned seminary C to develop "a program of in-depth studies in the gospel and formation for service and ministry in the

---

66. "Concluye el primer curso," para. 1.

churches," particularly for "those churches that do not have functioning programs, and they are wanting it."[67]

Seminary C was established during the time when seminaries A and B were transitioning to meet civil accreditation criteria, which included stipulated minimum academic qualifications for enrollment. Seminary C chose an alternative route to facilitate open access to theological education. It sought less demanding academic recognition outside of Spain with an established European nonformal theological program within its own denominational network. Three professors who had been serving as faculty at Seminary B (all members of Anabaptist/Mennonite denominations) joined together to initiate and give administrative direction to the new seminary.

The Physical Context

Seminary C has neither a campus nor a designated permanent administrative space. Although not owning or renting a physical location reduces expenses, seminary C cited not having a designated location as one of its weaknesses in a strengths, weaknesses, opportunities, and threats (SWOT) analysis in 2018.[68] They typically meet in-person seven times a year for a day-long class offered one Saturday per month in a nondenominational evangelical church on the east side of Madrid. One of the three administrative faculty members grew up in that congregation, so the connection is relational rather than denominational. The church's location facilitates access by either car or public transportation for students who commute from various regions of Spain to the Saturday sessions. The facility includes an ample sanctuary with moveable chairs and portable tables that can be arranged to transform the space into a classroom setting or common dining area as needed. The seminary has been permitted to place a single tall, narrow bookshelf in a corner of the sanctuary that holds a small library for students.

The Virtual Context

The seminary's website serves as a central hub for asynchronous communication throughout the year; it maintains a virtual presence in Spain

67. "Centro Teológico Kenosis," para. 1–2.
68. Centro Teológico Koinonía, *SWOT*. This report was submitted to the OMS Theological Education Regional consultant in Madrid in 2018.

and beyond. The website communicates information about the seminary, course of study, and professors. The home page, however, is primarily used to post personalized up-to-date announcements from the professors to inform students about current or future courses. Students have access to the seminary's virtual learning environment (VLE), which houses the course materials, assignments, and recordings of class sessions, permitting course completion without physical attendance. The VLE, however, is not the primary means of formation for the learning community, but rather, the Saturday in-person class sessions.

The Relational Context

Seminary C is affiliated with Spain's AMyHCE churches, which endorse the seminary as the theological education provider for their pastors, ministry leaders, and congregants.[69] The institution is also recognized by the Mennonite Central Committee in Europe. One Mission Society (OMS), the mission with which I serve, has also partnered with the seminary to provide faculty and limited financial resources for student travel scholarships. As noted, the three administrators at seminary C have had faculty roles at seminary B, and one currently holds a faculty position there as well. The two institutions have a collaborative, yet unofficial, relationship that facilitates the sharing of seminary B's faculty as visiting lecturers and the use of its extensive library resources.

The Instructional Context

The seminary's 2012 promotional video states, seminary C is "more than a center of studies, it is formation in community, . . . a center where you share reflections, uncertainties, and life."[70] Antonio González, Rector C, believes that "theological formation is a communal process."[71] The practice of communal learning is a core feature of its educational design. The administrators appreciate the formative potential of dialogue during class and informal fellowship.

---

69. "Titulación," para. 4.
70. "Centro Teológico Koinonía (CTK)," 0.57–0.58, 1.04–1.06.
71. Antonio González was unavailable to be interviewed, so he is referenced by name rather than as Rector C to credit his published material. González, "Cinco años," para. 5.

By 2014 the seminary had ninety-five students registered for the course of study, yet the average Saturday attendance was nineteen, so only 20 percent of those who were enrolled participated in the Saturday classes.[72] In 2018, it celebrated the first graduation with three students completing the five-year course of study. In April 2020, it reported a total enrollment of 148 students with an average of thirty-four attending the Saturday sessions, or 23 percent. Only four students were added to the matriculated total by April 2021.[73] The average percentage of actual participation remained close to 20 percent. The graduation rate based on these enrollment numbers is slightly above 2 percent.

Reflecting on the increasing number of matriculated students, one can conclude that the community of faith has an interest in theological formation. The transition from interest to a decision to complete a degree is either infrequent or requires additional time beyond the seminary's five-year cyclical design. Cost is not an obstacle; students pay a minimal fee when they attend a Saturday class, and their transportation can be reimbursed.[74] Failure to attend a class has no financial or enrollment consequences. The ease of access captivates interest but may fail to communicate the seriousness of the program as a complete course of study rather than an *a la carte* selection of individual courses.

The administrators have designed an instructional model that combines online and in-person learning to facilitate access to the course of study for congregants and ministry leaders from across Spain, particularly for those coming from AMyHCE churches. Although its decision to function without a dedicated permanent physical location provides flexibility and reduces expenses, it leaves the seminary vulnerable to having to seek alternative meeting venues and limits the types of tangible resources that it can provide, including its physical or in-person availability to students.

---

72. González, "Anabaptist Theology Formation Centre," sec. 1.

73. Seminary C, email messages to OMS/researcher, Apr. 21, 2020, Feb. 3, 2021.

74. When this case study was conducted in 2018, students paid ten euros for each class.

Mission and Identity

Mission

Faculty C-1 stated the seminary's mission: "We want to serve for all of [a person's] life and to serve people, the normal, ordinary member of the church." His statement is confirmed on the seminary's website: "[Seminary C] does not want to form elites, but rather to serve Christian churches where they actually find themselves."[75] González specified their program is designed to serve "youth, elderly, pastors, non-pastors, men, and women with [diverse] levels of secular education, [from] distinct professions, very diverse nationalities, and with the most variety of vital and church experiences."[76] Although the administrators affirm that ministry leaders and teachers have greater necessity of formation because of their responsibility to lead others, they have designed the format of the program to facilitate its accessibility to the wider faith community.[77] According to González, this emphasis on theological literacy for all believers is rooted in historic Anabaptist theological understandings and practice.[78] It also bears resemblance to the design of theological education in the early church, the Jerusalem or missional model.

One of the ways the seminary demonstrates its commitment to accessibility is through an open-admission policy. It welcomes students with or without formal studies or certificates. This inclusivity characterizes the Saturday classes, which have many non-credit seeking students enrolled, occasional visitors who are welcomed as fully participating auditors for the day, and a small number of students who submit course assignments for credit. This reality is represented in its statistics, which show increasing enrollment—however, with few pursuing credits towards graduation.

Although inclusive admission standards facilitate accessibility, the resulting diversity in cultural backgrounds and entering levels of educational formation necessitate that professors take each student's level of ability into consideration when evaluating the work. Seminary C's SWOT acknowledges the accommodation of "differing levels of academic ability" as a threat.[79] The implication of this contextual reality is that although faculty

---

75. "Quienes somos," CTK, para 3.
76. González, "Cinco años," para. 7.
77. González and Rosell, "CTK," q. 3.
78. González, "Cinco años," para. 10.
79. Centro Teológico Koinonía, "SWOT."

may present theologically specialized scholarly materials, those materials and related assignments must be accompanied with generalized explanations and individualized grading.

The seminary offers an educational service to the churches, which are the ones, they believe, who have the primary responsibility for the formation of their members.[80] Its broad recruitment design to reach the entire faith community, rather than a more specialized focus on equipping ministry leaders, suggests their commitment to supplement the formation offered in local churches.

When asked to share a representative story of the successful fulfilment of its mission, faculty C-1 told the story of one of the nontraditional matriculated students:

> She is a woman with few studies. . . . She has finished five years [the diploma level] and now is in her seventh year, and still, she has an incredible interest. A person that perhaps they don't value much in the church because she doesn't speak well, doesn't have an academic level, but nevertheless the seminary has been, for her, part of her Christian discipleship, and it has helped her to come out of herself, to have more confidence, to have a study group with other women and to come alongside of people.

Faculty C-1 references a critical element of the seminary's mission, which is discipleship, the practice of equipping individuals to follow and obey Jesus Christ.

The Course of Study

The source of seminary C's course of study is the program Formation Biblique Pour le Service Dans L'Eglise (FBSE) developed in and for the context of Mennonite Swiss and French churches by the Center de Formation et de Rencontre Bienenberg (CeFoR). FBSE offers nonformal theological formation designed to educate and train people who remain in their local churches. The course of study presents a broad-spectrum overview of "six disciplines of theology," including doctrine, ethics, church history, practical service, biblical studies, and exegesis/hermeneutics and is designed to be completed over a five-year cycle of thirty-five courses, with seven taught each year.[81] According to the FBSE website,

80. González and Rosell, "CTK," q. 5.
81. These six areas are specified in the French language student manual of FBSE.

> The [complete] training represents the amount of teaching hours equivalent to one semester of a normal session at a Bible institute. This permits [students]: to cover all the important areas of theology (knowledge), to acquire skills for service in the Church (know-how), and to develop a responsible Christian life (interpersonal skills).

Although this program is much less comprehensive than the accredited bachelor's degrees offered by seminaries A and B (covering in total the equivalent of just one of their semesters), it is suited to the current contextual needs of the AMyHCE churches, which recognize it as their denominational theological training program in Spain. Students may enter the cycle at any point because there are no prerequisites. Completion depends on whether students progress systematically through the entire curriculum or take courses intermittently. They may elect to earn a certificate for either one or three years of attendance, validated by a final oral exam. A diploma is offered for those who complete the full cycle, successfully submit all relevant coursework and readings, and pass a final oral exam. Course materials are distributed to registered students via the VLE portal one month prior to the Saturday class. The brevity of time given to instruction (one day of in-person instruction and ten hours of independent work) does not lend itself to a level of development in ministry practices, theological wisdom, or biblical understanding that are typically sought by or expected of those seeking ministerial leadership formation.

Identity

Seminary C's faith heritage, Anabaptist and Mennonite, informs and shapes its theology, identity, practices, and church affiliations. According to González, the emphases on personal piety, community, pacificism, and the exercise of spiritual gifts introduce distinctive and needed forms of Christian practice into the current context of Spain's Protestantism.[82] However, the greater Protestant community is represented in the faculty and student body.

Seminary C, like seminaries A and B, expects its faculty members to have postgraduate academic qualifications and/or have demonstrated work or ministry experience in the disciplines that they teach. Their academic

---

"FBSE," 7, 12–13.

82. González and Rosell, "Mucho que decir," 7:27—11:18.

qualifications lend credibility to the institution. The three administrators and the visiting professors serve voluntarily, relying on supplemental income or other employment. This is another factor contributing to the minimal cost of matriculation. However, it also means that the administrators and lecturers are bi-vocational with no one giving their full time to the maintenance, relationships, and development of the institution. The seminary's identity, as expressed through the faculty's example of service, appears to serve as a living example of the practicing learning community envisioned in seminary C's mission statement.

Pervasive Scarcity

Pervasive scarcity is one of the greatest challenges to seminary C's ability to fulfil its mission. Faculty C-1 noted, "Always the scarcity, the scarcity in relation to means." The seminary experiences limitations in available time, facilities, personnel, technology, and the extension of its educational reach. Faculty C-1 commented,

> At times the lack of being able to dedicate more time, of not having the structure with an office with many people dedicated to do—to be able to, for example all of the courses that we are giving—to do them in video format [and] audio, to make them available in a format for South America, all the Spanish speaking world. We have some money, but we do not have enough people to do that much work.

Faculty C-1 substantiates his outward looking vision despite severely limited resources. "I believe that [the seminary] is a program that is functioning well. . . . This burdens me that we cannot reach more people." He is satisfied with the current design and practices. The aim is to offer nonformal Hispanophone theological education to as many as possible. Vision and confidence can fuel innovation, yet seminary C must also work within the context of scarcity. The part-time reality of seminary C's administrators, faculty, and students is a critical inhibiting factor in the realization of its vision for Spain and beyond.

The Contextualization of the Curriculum

Contextual Responsiveness

Seminary C shares historical European Mennonite theological convictions and practices, yet faces the contextual challenges of adapting the instruction to address the unique needs, question, and circumstances of the church in Spain.[83] The seminary's agreement with CeFoR, gives the administrators permission to "[adapt the course of study] to the needs of the Spanish-speaking Mennonite Churches."[84] The specification of this target group reveals an important point. The distinctives of this denomination are to be primary in the contextualization of seminary C's formation.

Faculty C-1 stressed, however, that the seminary attends to the contextualization of the course materials by observing the context of Spain and the Spanish evangelical church in general.

> [Seminary C] is a program that comes from Switzerland where it was tested over many years. And [what] we have done, ourselves, is adapt, not so much the [plan of study], [but] the [course] material that we give based on the [plan of study]. We have a basic title for each [course] and we try to prepare it, conforming it to the needs of the church in Spain, and for Spain.

He illustrated this practice with an example of how they decided to insert a new course into the existing plan of study. "We realized that a great part of the churches in Spain divide over problems of leadership and internal problems. Therefore immediately we formed a course about mediation. We try to respond to what we see." The fact that they recognize ecclesial or societal issues that are contextually necessary to address indicates their intention to practice cultural responsiveness. The illustration of the course on mediation demonstrates that although it may be reactive rather than proactive, the response was immediate. He also noted, as did both seminaries A and B, their freedom to select course content. "We have sufficient liberty to give the content of the courses that we want."

My first teaching experience at the seminary illustrates this liberty. In preparation for teaching, I was given a course title, "The Helping Relationship," and instructed to post an introductory assignment in the Moodle

83. "Centro Teológico Kénosis," para. 7.

84. This "protocole d'accord" was received from a representative of the Bienenberg Center de Formation. Bienenberg Center de Formation, email message to researcher, June 9, 2020, translated using Google Translate.

platform one month prior to the course; plan the instruction for the day-long Saturday class, allowing for two coffee breaks and the midday meal; and finally post the final assignment(s) for course credit after the Saturday session. The course title alone was unhelpful to me, so I requested a course description. I was then given a brief paragraph in French, the FBSE's description of the course, which indicated that it was typically taught by someone with a background in psychology. The administrators of seminary C told me that I could develop the course according to what I thought would be best but always with reference to the given course title. The FBSE curricula framework is the critical point of reference. It provides a scaffold that seminary C can then fill in as contextually appropriate. Finding materials in Spanish proved to be a difficult task. I had to adjust based on the available Spanish resources, and that was an exercise in contextualization. I delivered the course based on my research on the helping relationship—the relationship between a caregiver, such as a pastor, and the one who receives help. Seminary C's administrators were satisfied, but whether I had met FBSE's objectives remained unknown.

The selection of lecturers represents another form of contextual responsiveness. Faculty C-1 noted, "We [the three administrators] are the people who invite the [lecturers]. . . . We develop the topics together with [CeFoR]. We are attentive to the students and we coordinate." They bring their first-hand knowledge, experiences, and perspectives as Spaniards to their preparation of course materials, selection of lecturers, and to their chosen methods of instruction, a contextualization practice cited by all three seminaries in this study.

All classes are offered in Spanish. Consequently, non-Spanish faculty have experienced linguistic immersion and, with few exceptions, live and work in Spain. There are risks involved in the reliance on itinerant faculty, such as variations in the level of instruction or ability to communicate. However, the three administrators maintain instructional control, generally delivering the majority of the seven courses each year. They also attend and participate in every class, even when they are not instructing.

Evaluation and Informal Feedback

The three administrators meet annually to evaluate each year's seven course series and to adjust for the next year. Faculty C-1 commented that they have had little success collecting formalized feedback due to a low rate of return of student surveys. They have opted for a more informal qualitative method to gather feedback. "The evaluation we do . . . [is] also within each course. We talk with the students and eat with the students." He described this informal feedback as the "living voice" of the students. This approach is consistent with their practice of a communal environment and table fellowship, but what was not clarified was the process for formulating questions, documenting results, and analysis. Students would not have the option of anonymity in this present practice. Without a systematic plan for recording the feedback, it could be forgotten, and the reliability of the data would rely on the memory of the hearer. The potential for bias or gaps could potentially diminish its value as a source for contextual adjustments, yet they value the practice and fruits of listening.

Student Perspectives

Two students, both active members in their local churches, independently highlighted the personal rather than vocational or academic value of their formation. Student C-1 spoke about personal and social transformation. "It has helped me a great deal to grow as a person. . . . My form of being and character have changed much with other people in my environment, with my family, in my home. It is a tremendous change." Student C-2 twice described the formative impact of her studies as "nourishment." She, like students at seminary A, spoke about the impact of relearning knowledge she had forgotten and of new learning about the Christian faith.

> [The professors] have reaffirmed my experiences, of my time past. They have refreshed many things that you knew but they had remained wrapped up. . . . I was listening to things that would not only refresh but they would amplify my knowledge and others of the things that I had never heard before, novelties. . . . Something that you say, "I have never heard this before in my life." . . . Therefore, to me, I like it and it challenges me.

She also shared an example of how her studies have shaped her professional life.

> After listening to the topic about creation and evolution by two . . . scientists by profession, . . . I decided that my primary classes in the school [where I was teaching] would be different. I have totally changed the exposition of the topic—that is very controversial

above all in [a particular] community—but I am not going to return to give the topic as I did before.

These students are responding to discipleship, as described by faculty C-1. The prioritization of a formation that is offered to all students reflects the Anabaptist and Mennonite emphasis on the priesthood of all believers.[85]

The students generally expressed satisfaction with the relevance of the course materials. They did, however, suggest new topics for the curriculum. Student C-1 said, "I would like more [instruction about] how to interact with people, . . . a course to learn how to reach people." This was a contextual need also voiced by seminary A's students. Student C-2 had several ideas:

> I believe that it would be interesting to do a type of study that would help us to go more deeply into the Muslim life and beliefs because I believe that we have many mistaken things. . . . Because when you know the people, it helps you not to reject them.
>
> [More] knowledge of the Word. Perhaps in my environment, what is the study of the Word shines because of its absence, but biblical illiteracy exists among the youngest [people] of our churches.
>
> I am also especially interested in house churches. I have heard and read about this topic, and it has renewed my hope.

Their suggestions are rooted in their context. They want to be more skilled in communicating with those around them, to be more familiar with the different people groups who live within Spain, to address biblical illiteracy, especially among the younger generations, and to be equipped to address weaknesses or possibilities for growth within the Spanish evangelical church.

Formalizing a method for recording stories and feedback would provide a way to evaluate contextual relevance as well as successes and failures in the completion of aims. If the current plan of studies developed in Switzerland does not address the topics identified by students or local congregations in Spain, evidence from such feedback strengthens arguments for the creation of new courses.

---

85. Espinoza, "Pia Desideria," 143.

Accreditation

Seminary C considers the protocol agreement with CeFoR to be the basis for its academic recognition. This agreement establishes the framework for the course of study, provides a minimal measure of accountability, and offers a diploma that opens some limited pathways to continuing education. Unlike seminaries A and B, seminary C is not civilly accredited nor has it sought accreditation through an agency such as the European Council of Theological Accreditation (ECTE). Civil or ECTE accreditation would hold the seminary to more stringent terms of governance and educational practices. The 2018 SWOT cited the following as weaknesses: "We do not have an additional level of licensure above what we offer. . . . We are not recognized by the Spanish government. We are not a legal entity."[86] These statements suggest recognition of civil accreditation's value. However, the seminary's commitment to theologically form all people, to allow open access regardless of previous academic experience, and to provide inexpensive formation have been determining factors in its accreditation choices. The part-time voluntary status of the administrators and faculty are not conducive to fulfilling the typical standards of accreditation for institutions of higher learning. However, the opportunity to partner with the greater European Mennonite community provides support and a network of institutions with which it can dialogue and potentially form agreements for the acceptance of its diploma, a critical issue for students desiring further education.

According to the protocol agreement, CeFoR will recognize seminary C's curriculum if it demonstrates that it has followed FBSE's established course of study.[87] Faculty C-1 explained the guidelines for adherence to the FBSE course of study.

> The courses, the subjects are designed with Bienenberg [CeFoR] and they can give to us accreditation, and we have to give the same relation to the pensum but what we do change is the content. We adapt it to our situation. And what weight do we have? A great deal. . . . We give so much liberty to the professor but always within

---

86. Centro Teológico Koinonía, "SWOT."

87. A representative of CeFoR described the accreditation relationship with seminary C as "an internal agreement between our two institutions, which stipulates that we, as the French-speaking department of Bienenberg, accredit [seminary C's] program to the level of one of our programs, called Biblical Training for Service in the Church (FBSE)." Bienenberg Center de Formation, email message to researcher, June 9, 2020.

the structure that we have with Bienenburg so that we are able to have accreditation.

He began this statement with the term *acreditación*, and ended it with *acreditación*. Although this academic recognition may have significantly less weight in the context of higher education, it is a relationship that the seminary values and seeks to maintain.

Seminary C's website has a dedicated page that explains its academic relationship and agreements. It mentions the source of the course of study, FBSE, and then describes the program's design by French and Swiss churches in connection with Bienenberg Theological Seminary and with the French-speaking CeFoR nonformal program with which it has its original protocol agreement.[88] The protocol agreement does not include stipulations for accreditation visits, institutional governance or assessment policies, collection of student feedback, samples of work, or established core competencies. This recognition does not compare to the extensive civil accreditation standards of ANECA that seminaries A and B observe. However, when seminary C celebrated its first student graduation, CeFoR sent a representative from Switzerland to participate in the ceremony, a visible demonstration of their commitment to the protocol agreement.[89] Their shared faith heritage prioritizes relationship. This arrangement allows seminary C flexibility to function inexpensively and to prioritize serving AMyHCE churches. Although the administrators of seminary C are theologians and academics, their decision to conduct nonformal theological education highlights the seminary's aim to offer theological education to all the church.

Church Relations

The seminary's affiliated denomination, AMyHCE, lists thirteen congregations in Spain dispersed among five provinces (Vigo, Cataluña, Girona, Burgos and Madrid).[90] Like the IEE, it too is a minority within Spain's minority evangelical population. As members of that denomination, the three administrators' relationships with these churches are personal and direct, facilitated by annual denominational gatherings and the ease of

---

88. "Titulación," para. 2–3.
89. Faculty C-1, email message to researcher, Oct. 8, 2019.
90. "Nuestras comunidades en España."

travel to these provinces. Faculty C-1 said, "The students that we have are from local churches that we know; we are forming them. We see that we are part of local churches."

Although the AMyHCE community forms the nucleus of seminary C, the faculty and students represent a diversity of Protestant denominations. The faculty, in particular, model church engagement and service through personal involvement as pastors, teachers, and in other ministries, such as counseling or mediation. This is a practical approach to address the barriers between the church and the seminary, a challenge addressed similarly by seminaries A and B. Faculty C-1 said,

> We have requested more support from the churches. . . . In the end, what [has] occurred is what always happens, [the churches] leave it to us to do [theological education] because we are the specialists. But as all of us are pastors we are involved in a way we can [do] this. We would like more participation from the [churches], but we are the ones who have to encourage it.

Faculty C-1's observation suggests that the church, represented by both its leaders or the full congregation, may not understand or appreciate the service that the seminary seeks to provide to them. Despite the faculty's incarnational participation in the churches, they recognize the existence of a perceived distinction between the church and the academy, an observation noted earlier by Rector A. This perception challenges efforts to form a mutual partnership.

Positively, Faculty C-1 highlighted the role that students play as catalysts in the development of healthy relationships between the church leadership and the seminary. The students may not be primary gatekeepers, but they are like side doors, connecting the church to the seminary in a two-way flow of exchange. Faculty C-1 noted,

> Some of the people from Burgos, who did not come in the beginning, come now because their children . . . came and liked it, and they encouraged others. This does not only have repercussions for [the seminary gaining students but] later they ask us to go to other churches to teach and to become involved with them.

Weaknesses in Spain's Protestant Church

Like seminaries A and B, seminary C acknowledges the overall weakness of the Spanish Protestant church. Faculty C-1 commented, "In Spain everything that you do at a ministry level [in or with the church] is pioneer"—meaning, start at the beginning or as yet undeveloped. This encapsulates the struggle of Spain's Protestant church to thrive. Seminary C, in spite of its highly qualified faculty, functions with minimal resources and limited periods of direct involvement with students. Consequently, the seminary's ability to build momentum in both the number of people it can theologically train and the thoroughness of that formation is impeded.

Faculty C-1 noted the church's financial weakness in relation to equipping people for church ministry.

> There are people called to ministry, perhaps full time, but the circumstances in Spain are not such right now that they can dedicate themselves to it. This has to do not so much with the seminary but the social precariousness of the churches.

With few financially sustainable career opportunities for pastoral ministry, seminary C's decision to equip the "ordinary members" responds to the current overall reality of the church. The seminary is working to fill a niche by prioritizing theological formation for the entire faith community.

Reflecting on the church, student C-2 said,

> It is very complicated to work in the Spanish evangelical church [long pause with several sighs and exhales of breath].... I believe that if we put ourselves, how do you say it, put ourselves in plan, "It is like this, like this, like this," it is very difficult to approach people.... It is to say, "What the Bible says is very literal. This has to be like this. It has always been like this." This tendency at times, so conservative, that I see in many evangelical brethren, I believe it does not help to approach people ... and each time less in the society in which we actually live.

According to her perception, the church's reactionary rigidity holds the church fixed in past doctrinal teachings and practices and hinders it from engagement with those who do not observe or practice faith as it does. This impacts its openness and ability to make theological contextual adjustments. This likely exacerbates the Protestant church's minority status, encircling it in a narrow theological bubble.

However, seminary C is working to break that bubble or at least reduce the number of people within it. Student C-2 shared how the faculty are introducing her to information that challenges her perspectives. They create a safe communal space to discuss a range of topics. She shared,

> One of the comments that [the rector] has made [in a Saturday session], when he was speaking of this problem that exists in [some countries] with their behaviors towards gay people, I have not heard an answer like [his]. . . . [Typically] we entangle ourselves in "No, no, no, you have to do this and this and this," but it seems very interesting to me, . . . to say what perspective do we have before all this wave. . . . It would be interesting if *before* we have a problem, to have some idea of where we are going to go, or at least to dialogue about this, talk, to clarify the ideas. (Emphasis original.)

This practice of theological reflection on contemporary questions and issues is valued by González who seeks to apply theological understanding to the discernment of a relevant and faithful response. He wrote,

> Instead of remaining bound by doctrinal chains, or by superficial fads, [seminary C] wants to be an environment of renewal where it is possible to open oneself intellectually to the figure of the same Messiah that was experienced and proclaimed by primitive Christianity and who continues alive today.[91]

Societal Engagement

When asked how seminary C is particularly designed for the context of Spain, faculty C-1 said, "Well, perhaps not so much Spain, but [for] Europe." He based this perspective on the curriculum's Swiss origin but did not elaborate on any distinctive European characteristics of the design or practices. A concern, also mentioned by seminary A's students, was voiced by student C-1. Communicating with people in the society, speaking with them in a way that opens dialogue is particularly challenging. She said,

> The culture is very, very, very hard, no? It is not like other cultures. . . . Therefore, I have to adapt myself to this culture in order to be able speak and to be able to initiate a conversation. . . . The people are very, very closed. They don't accept that you speak with them about the gospel. . . . According to the culture here they are more Catholic. But Catholics for religion. . . . Because they say, "I am not, I am not a practitioner. I am only Catholic."

Society's hardness juxtaposed with the "pioneer" status of the Protestant church highlights the degree of challenge presented to all three

---

91. González, "Cinco años," para. 4.

seminaries. Spain's society has a complex mixture of an increasingly nonreligious population, a diminishing, yet historically rooted Catholic population, and migrating populations with diverse faiths.

A review of the curriculum reveals that there are a significant number of courses designed to explore the values, practices, and current context of the society. The seminary's ability to offer relevant courses on current issues reflects its liberty and commitment to adapt the curriculum as needed because it is not encumbered by the requirements of a demanding accreditation body.

González offers a vision for societal engagement:

> It is necessary to respond to our civilization, in its artistic, scientific, philosophical, and technical plurality. . . . It requires that the plurality of reality is actualized in the very education, permitting students and professors to grow in wisdom that provides the plurality of shared abilities and the riches of the gifts of the Spirit.[92]

To put flesh on these words, theological education offered through a program that only meets seven Saturdays for a total of just over sixty hours per year would require extraordinary optimism and perseverance. It is a pioneer work of faith.

Seminary C and the Four Continua

Seminary C reflects its Anabaptist and Mennonite heritage in its commitment to accessible theological education and in its practice of communal learning. A protocol agreement with CeFoR Bienenberg provides it with an internally accredited course of study through the proven work and experience of FBSE. It has found a pathway to theologically form and empower the church, a church that has been consistently characterized as weak throughout the research data.

Seminary C's alignment on the four continua would be: *For whom is theological education?* Education for all the church rather than for a select few. *Which educational methodology is utilized?* Cognitive and experiential formation experienced in a learning community rather than a formal classroom or in-ministry training. *What is the aim or purpose?* Faith development and discipleship of the priesthood of believers emphasized over academic theological proficiency and professional clergy

---

92. González, "Cinco años," para 90.

development. And *where does the seminary locate itself in relation to church and society?* Although it offers in-person instruction delivered within a church building, the seminary itself has no physical presence in Spain. It has a relational presence with its affiliated denomination, and it has a digital presence in society through the website, designed primarily for its students. Its alignment reflects the teaching and practices of the Anabaptist and Mennonite heritage as it follows many aspects of the historical model of communal nonformal theological education practiced in the first centuries of the church.

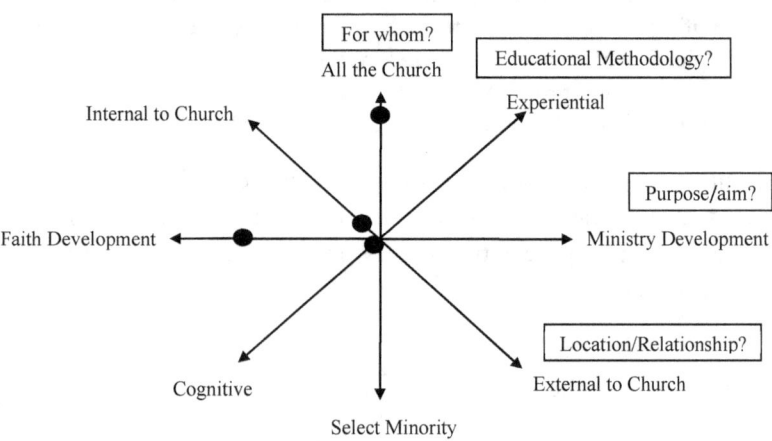

Figure 5 Seminary C Continua

Seminary C's lack of physical groundedness, low expenses, minimal personnel, and liberty to make contextual adaptations facilitate its ability to respond to educational opportunities as they arise. However, it lacks the balancing voices of an external board, a formal accrediting agency, or a formal advisory group of non-faculty pastors and congregants. The program is fueled by visionary idealism in spite of its limitations and capacity for growth. In comparison with the accredited formal education offered by seminaries A and B, seminary C's design and practices embody a nonformal approach to theological education for all the church.

Questions for Reflection on the Case Study of Seminary C

1. Keeping in mind the historical contexts of theological education and Spain's Protestants and the perspectives of the survey participants, in

what ways is seminary C adapting its designs and practices for the unique context of the church in Spain? Give two or three examples. What is missing or could be improved?

2. How could seminary C address the issue of student retention? Remember to consider their context and the reality of scarcity.

3. In your context, what is or what could be a design for informal theological education that would effectively equip the church?

A Final Comparison of the Three Seminaries

Seminary A has chosen to maintain a more traditional model of residential theological formation and works closely with its affiliated denomination. Of the three seminaries, it prioritizes ministerial formation and requires its students to serve in local churches as an integral component of their formation. It faces the challenge of relevance as it seeks to be both faithful and prophetic in the context of an increasingly diverse society. Seminary B has chosen to adapt in response to the financial and lifestyle realities of its students through its transition to a fully online program. It prioritizes scholarly theological formation balanced with spiritual care for its students. It faces the challenge of marginalization as it serves an ecumenical minority denomination and navigates the suspicion of the greater conservative Protestant evangelical community. Seminary C has chosen an alternative pathway, opting for nonformal formation that meets their commitment to accessibility. It has the greatest flexibility to contextualize its course offerings according to the needs of the church in Spain. It faces the challenge of student retention and the limitations of no full-time dedicated faculty or staff to extend the reach of their formation.

THE FRUITS OF LISTENING

Figure 6 Comparison of Three Seminary Continua

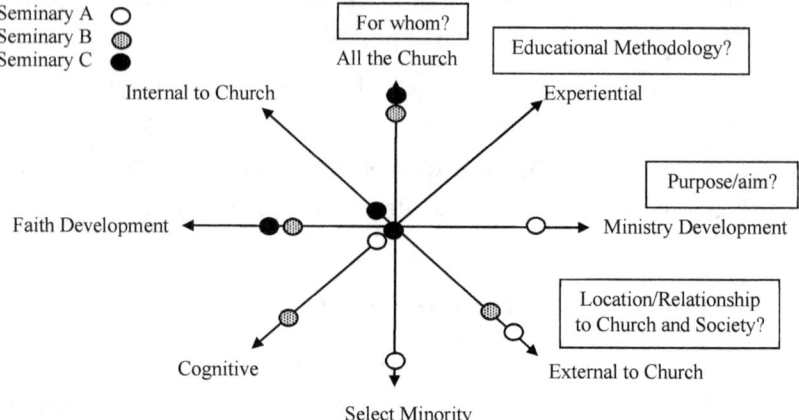

Questions for Reflection

1. What are the positive aspects of having three quite distinct seminaries functioning in a similar geographic context?

2. If you were to design a fourth seminary for Madrid, how would it differ from these three seminaries to address additional contextualization issues?

6

Harvesting the Fruits of Listening

> *In order to survive [theological education] needs to continually adapt to its environment without losing its integrity, and its vision, mission, and mandate. It is continually involved in maintaining a delicate balance between who it is and relevance to the context in which it lives.*
>
> —Rupen Das[1]

Fruit ripens over time, much like the process of doing research. Listening to faculty, students, and church attenders and reflecting on their historical contexts bore a variety of fruits. The research produced several critical observations and answers to initiating questions: What are the distinctive components of contextually shaped designs and practices in theological education? How are these contextually shaped designs and practices developed and then implemented? When contextualization is either not happening or is limited in its scope and application, what factors hinder its development, and what are the implications of those limitations? The three seminaries contextually engage to greater or lesser degrees with people in three distinct yet interconnected contexts: the institution itself, the church, and the society. They face challenges that test their resolve and capacity to remain faithful and to fulfil their mission to equip ministry leaders and to empower Spain's Protestant evangelical faith community to carry out the work of the church in their local contexts as well as in the world.

---

1. Das, *Connecting Curriculum with Context*, loc. 1316.

The research identified and critiqued two contextualization practices currently implemented by the seminaries. Based on the analysis of the data, the work proposes five additional contextualization practices that seminaries could leverage to evaluate the effectiveness of their designs and practices. Some additional challenges to contextualization are noted in the observations of how the seminaries are engaging with the church and society. Although the research was situated in Madrid, Spain, the likelihood of "transformative resonance" supports the criticality of communicating these observations to global theological educators involved in the work of contextualizing their institutional designs and practices for the diverse faith communities and societies in which they serve.[2]

Contextualization Practices and Challenges

Institutional Frameworks

Institutional frameworks are not without their foundational biases, particularly if they have been designed to function in a different cultural context. Whether they are exported or imported, components of the seminaries' designs, such as the institutional organization, mission, curriculum, and location, should be frequently evaluated for contextual relevance, the appropriateness of aims, and their continued effectiveness at facilitating educational objectives. Although the institutions have made some adjustments over the years, they continue to implement curricular designs that originated outside of Spain.

Seminaries A and B have courses of study that align with the fourfold encyclopedic design that was developed to equip students in four disciplines: Bible, theology, church history, and pastoral ministry. Since the publication of Farley's critique of that design, some scholars have disputed its effectiveness for equipping students to serve and empower the contemporary church.[3] Osmer points out the historical situatedness of the fourfold design; some of the problems it addressed in the modern period may no longer be relevant in a current postmodern context.[4] The study

---

2. Swinton and Mowat, *Practical Theology*, 45.

3. Scholars who have critiqued the fourfold model include Farley, *Theologia*; Ott, *Beyond Fragmentation*, 6; Shaw, *Transforming Theological Education*, 17–18; Aleshire, *Earthen Vessels*, loc. 468–476; Osmer, *Practical Theology*, 231, 234–255; Vanhoozer, "From Bible to Theology," 233.

4. Osmer, *Practical Theology*, 231, 234–235.

of the four disciplines is not in question here but rather the lack of their integration in the formation of the whole person. Cannell challenges the deficiencies of the fourfold design with a question:

> In order to foster the capacities of wise judgement, reflection, and theological reasoning; in order to help people sustain healthy relationships, relate truly to God, judge clearly among ethical alternatives, and offer the kind of leadership needed by the church in this age, does the fourfold model need to be revised—or abandoned altogether and a new structure created?[5]

Although Cannell is concerned with theological education primarily in the North American context, the concerns and weaknesses noted in her question resonate with the characteristics and practices for ministry leaders suggested by seminary A's students and by the parishioners who participated in the survey "Perspectives on Theological Education." They commented on the contextual importance of *acompañamiento*, virtue, personal spirituality, social engagement, and applied theological and biblical reflection. The implication of these critiques for Spain's theological education are that the fourfold design may be doubly ineffective; on one hand, it may have the noted weaknesses of an outdated model, ill-equipped for the formation of postmodern pastors and ministry leaders. On the other hand, having been designed for a different cultural context, it may not be well suited for the unique contextual distinctives facing the church and society in Spain.

Seminary C chose to import a different design, a model of informal theological education that had originated in Switzerland. The cyclical framework of its curricular design presents an opportunity for a more integrated learning experience. They alternate courses from various disciplines in each year's cycle. For example, the courses for 2024–25 included Muslims, Doctrines of Humanity and Creation, Ethics of Work, Questions of Life and Death, Church Planting and Growth, Ministry with Children and Youth, and Eschatology.[6] The courses offered in 2023–24 were The Holy Spirit: Gifts and Ministries, Family Ethics and Couples and Sexuality, History of the Reformation, Dynamics of the Early Church, No to Active Violence, The Christian Worship Service, and Old Testament: Prophets and History and Geography.[7] However, in their current format, inconsistent

---

5. Cannell, *Theological Education Matters*, 306–7.
6. Centro Teológica Koinonía, "Cursos del año 2024–2025."
7. Centro Teológica Koinonía, "Cursos del año 2023–2024."

attendance, guest lecturers, month-long gaps between courses, and the brevity of learning hours pose challenges for faculty and students to form a comprehensive overview of theological and practical connections between courses.

Scarcity: A Pervasive Challenge to Contextualization

The theme and reality of pervasive scarcity was present in each seminary case study even though the seminaries are situated in a cosmopolitan European capital city. Scarcity has become a "root metaphor" in the stories of these seminaries; it is the lens that focuses, filters, or distorts how they perceive the present and consider future possibilities.[8] The ecclesial context of scarcity in which these institutions function affects their finances, available personnel, time, and material resources. These deficits complicate, slow, or prevent some of the contextual adaptations that they would like to make—for example, updating technology and library resources, paying faculty competitive salaries, expanding their program to reach a wider audience, or planning for the future without fear that there will be no funds to operate. The weight and constancy of scarcity factors into their designs and practices.

Theologically and biblically, contentment and perseverance are countermeasures when faced with diminished resources and other obstacles; they are evidence of faith anchored in Christ.[9] Although scarcity is a formidable challenge, the case studies highlighted several positive lessons that can be learned from the examples of these seminaries: Scarcity requires a willingness to make personal sacrifices. It encourages stewardship of resources. It is best faced as a team. It teaches us "to not always privilege the urgent." It facilitates the acceptance of limitations. It does not need to weaken commitment to one's call, and it does not determine worth, expertise, nor identity.

Two Identified Contextualization Practices

Two contextualization practices emerged from the analysis of the case studies. The seminaries can implement these inexpensive methods and

---

8. Vanhoozer, "Everyday Theology," 52.
9. Phil 4:11–13, 19; Rom 5:3–5; Jas 1: 2–4.

adapt theological formation without having to make substantial alterations to their current designs.

1. Contextualization Through Indigenous Faculty

All three seminaries rely on their indigenous faculty to contextualize the course of study, regardless of its source. Their utilization of this contextualization practice aligns with one of Bevans's six models of contextual theology, the anthropological model, in which the knowledge and experiences of the people in the receiving community adapt and adjust the message for the local context.[10] The indigenous population, according to the anthropological model, understands the unwritten and unspoken aspects of the culture—its memories, dreams, frustrations, and regional distinctives. The seminaries' indigenous faculty apply their experiential knowledge and understanding as members of the Spanish church and Spanish society to contextualize curricular designs, practices, and instruction.

There were several gaps, however, in the contextualization process. No specific references to or evidence of a systematic plan for conducting indigenous contextualization were identified. There was scarce or no mention of how they evaluate indigenous contextualization for subjectivity or blind spots, nor how the institutions adapt this practice when courses are taught by nonindigenous faculty. The contextual insights of indigenous professors would be limited by the scope of their own individual life experiences. Seminary A's students, who appreciate the contextualized explanations of the indigenous faculty, mentioned inconsistencies in the abilities and effectiveness of the practice from instructor to instructor. A transferrable process for applying indigenous contextualization would be critical for consistency if this continues to be a preferred practice. Increasing ethnic diversity in the churches will also challenge the effectiveness of reliance on indigenous contextualization, especially as it becomes increasingly critical to equip students for multiethnic ministry within Spain.

2. Contextualization through Control of Content

The second contextualization practice that the seminaries rely on is their liberty to select content for the courses listed in the curriculum. Faculty at

---

10. Bevans, *Models of Contextual Theology*, 55–56.

all three institutions commented on their power to choose content to ensure contextual relevance, to preserve theological faithfulness, and to exert their independence within the framework of their current curricular designs.

Selection of content comes with its own contextualization challenges. The breadth of Spain's indigenous evangelical scholarly resources is limited although Spain does have the benefit of published indigenous and respected Catholic scholarship that is available to Protestants who are amenable to including those resources. Sometimes the institutions select content that either requires that students be able to read in another language or that the institution must expend its limited resources to translate. Some imported content has been translated into Spanish. However, if it is only available in Latin American Spanish, rather than Castilian Spanish, there can be critical semantic and cultural differences embedded within the text that need to be contextualized for Spain. A positive aspect of appropriating content from the wider Protestant academic community is that it introduces students to the global Protestant community. However, utilization of imported content can perpetuate the influence of external cultures, their issues, and perspectives, which may be different from the concerns and issues of Spain's Protestants.

The seminaries' reliance on the selection of content as a contextualization practice suggests that they are appropriating a variation of Bevans's translation model; the Christian biblical message is believed to be supracontextual and divinely commissioned; consequently, the spoken or written translation of that message into the local dialect or language is considered sufficient for its contextual appropriation.[11] Content, however, is not transmitted as pure thought but with culturally embedded beliefs, perspectives, and practices. Inadvertently, uncontextualized exported or imported content could influence students' thinking, expectations, and behaviors through exposure to the beliefs and practices of other societies. As with indigenous contextualization, establishing a systematic process for the evaluation and adaptation of content would be prudent for contextually appropriate curricular design and practices. Teaching students how to practice theological, biblical, and critical discernment will equip them with tools to appreciate and understand the content and its original context and to then adapt its transmission, if needed, to serve the needs of the local church.

---

11. Bevans, *Models of Contextual Theology*, 43.

Contextualization Practices: Five Fruits Gathered through Listening

Five contextualization practices emerged from listening and reflecting on all the input that was shared and gathered. Each approach to contextualization is integrally grounded in the contexts of the Protestant evangelical seminaries, church, and society of Spain. The themes, challenges, and questions that they seek to address should resonate with churches, theological institutions, organizations, or even individuals who are seeking to communicate effectively, to understand why things are done as they are, to address challenges like scarcity, or to keep pace in a rapidly changing world. Implementation of these practices requires an investment of time and resources, reflection, and analysis; receptivity to listening to others; willingness to build new relationships; and openness to adjust designs and practices while simultaneously balancing doctrinal, institutional, or personal faithfulness with responsive contextual relevance.

The Fruit of Critical Remembering

Discovering the theological implications of one's unique historical context and how those implications shape current beliefs and practices is the work of critical remembering and practical theological reflection. Historical review and analysis can uncover forgotten or unacknowledged events, patterns, or beliefs that may shape the current attitudes, relationships, and actions of individuals or of communities. Critical reflection and discernment applied to the implications of historical discoveries can facilitate the evaluation of an individual's or community's faithfulness to its expressed or desired aims and beliefs. Reorientation, correction, healing, and freedom to move forward with new purpose and understanding are possible outcomes of critical remembering.

Given the role of the Roman Catholic Church in the history and current context of Spain, the infrequency of references to Catholicism, with the exception of a few comments in the survey and seminary B's ecumenical collaboration with Catholics, was intriguing. There were slightly more references to Islam, primarily in the context of current immigration trends. The main topic of conversation was the river of multiple currents running through the evangelical faith community and the challenges that the seminaries and ministry leaders face to faithfully navigate the raging river of shifting trends. Yet, sometimes what is not said speaks louder than audible words.

Intentional listening helped to identify several themes, or "root metaphors," that repeatedly emerged throughout the data: fragility, marginality, scarcity, and the Spanish Protestants' need to validate their legitimacy.[12] People retold narratives of past oppression, a historic "power interest," and they spoke of its ongoing effects, a reality that seemed to be perceived as the status quo.[13] As Drelichman et al. noted, "Nobody expects the Spanish Inquisition to still matter today, but it does."[14] One conversation alone would likely not call attention to the narratives of scarcity, fragility and legitimacy, but as the voices came together in the data, the reverberation of those themes indicated the present power of the past. Living in Spain taught me many things about the people and culture, both past and present, but intentional listening impressed me with the need to go deeper in my comprehension of what I was hearing. Critical remembering opened a new perspective on who people are, why they continue to tell the same narratives, and what restrains them from making changes.

Seminaries can educate their students in the practice of transformative theological reflection on the historical context of the people, places, and churches they are serving. The parishioners, faculty, and students suggested several courses and practices that could initiate a process of intentional listening, theological reflection, and critical remembering, including studies in Roman Catholicism, the history of Spain, Spanish culture, and the Reformation. The practices that they suggested would address long-held suspicions and fear through theological formation, collaboration with Catholic scholars, and increased personal engagement with the local community. The seminaries may not yet recognize the value of engaging the past to transform the present, but the contextualization practice of critical remembering offers them a resource towards the creation of a new narrative of who they are and where they are going. This is an outsider's analysis based on what was heard, a "counterpoint" to what is and what could be.[15]

---

12. Vanhoozer, "Everyday Theology," 52.
13. Vanhoozer, "Everyday Theology," 50–51.
14. Drelichman et al., "Long-Run Effects," 1.
15. Bevans, *Models of Contextual Theology*, 20.

The Fruit of Keeping Pace with Society

Intentionally equipping seminary students or church parishioners with the understanding and necessary skills to fearlessly theologically reflect on and address unique culturally situated societal challenges presents another opportunity to develop relevant contextualized theological formation. Societal issues that surfaced as concerns were dysfunctional families, human sexuality, generational differences, political developments, the environment, and immigration. The students spoke of their frustration, and one voiced fear, that their theological formation would not prepare them to respond to these contextual needs. In both the survey and student interviews, people expressed their desire to learn how to communicate more effectively with individuals in society. Although Rector A acknowledged that many of these issues are currently elements of reflection, it was noted that the seminary progresses slowly in its response to society, even more slowly than the church does. The fourfold design leaves little space for the practice of theological reflection on societal engagement and contemporary issues, but that is what students and the church are requesting. If faculty and students can consider these elements of reflection together and apply their findings through joint interactions with the local community, seminary A may find itself moving towards a new design of theological education, contextualized for the reality of Spain, a model that could be transported by students to the churches.

Seminary B is connecting with society by facilitating the formation of an ecumenical community of Catholics, Protestants, and non-confessing society members in a country with historic and ongoing religious persecution. However, its practice of interfaith collaboration "is not [viewed] with good eyes" by many in the evangelical community. Although the seminary serves a small denomination that sends few ministerial candidates and finds itself marginalized by conservative evangelicals, it remains committed to maintaining a design and practices that appeal to the theologically curious whatever their faith background may be. The time may have come to consider a revision of three aspects of the institutional design represented in the continua: For whom is theological education? What is the aim or purpose? What methodology can incorporate both rigor and faith?

Seminary C emphasizes an Anabaptist pacifism in a country that has been prone to terrorism. The seminary has an opportunity to model a contextualized theological response to violence. González recognizes this as one of the seminary's unique and important contributions to Spain's

Protestant church, but it is also a position that would likely be appealing to many in the society.[16] To share this position of peace with a wider audience, the seminary may need to consider adaptations to its design that would enable it to reach beyond the more insular context of the small denominational community and its Saturday learning communities.

Seminary A's students' desires for effective societal engagement, seminary B's ecumenical dialogues, and seminary C's example of pacificism present opportunities for applied contextual theology. However, their retelling of the narratives of fragility, scarcity, and marginality likely challenge their thinking and efforts towards societal engagement. Two of Bevans's models offer frameworks that could be adapted by the seminaries to facilitate societal engagement: the praxis model seeks to promote transformational change in the society through action, and the countercultural model emphasizes the transformative power of the proclaimed gospel message.[17] The implementation of either option will require designs and practices that encourage outward facing theological reflection that keeps pace with society and engagement with people in the society.

The Fruit of Accreditation as Contextual Engagement

Embracing the oversight of accrediting agencies, particularly those functioning within the same cultural context, facilitates a measure of educational contextualization within the institutions as they adapt their designs and practices to align with accreditation requirements. Although alignment increases the regulatory burden, the relationship opens channels of communication with the accrediting agency and with other accredited institutions. Through the relationship, institutions are exposed to different contextually situated perspectives that can provide a frame of reference for the evaluation of their own institutions.

Seminaries A and B have adapted their designs and many of their practices to Spain's norms of higher education. Civil accreditation, in the context of contextualization, holds these two seminaries accountable to Spain's established measures of educational quality assurance, external standards of governance, objective aims for student competencies, and the practice of inclusivity that requires the admission of qualified candidates regardless of their faith affiliation. Seminary B's emphasis on academic

---

16. González and Rosell, "Mucho que decir," 8:50—9:13.
17. Bevans, *Models of Contextual Theology*, 70, 120–21.

excellence aligns well with this rigor. Seminary A watchfully preserves its vocational and denominational priorities. Seminary C has entered a less demanding relationship with a validating institution outside of Spain but from its own denomination. Fewer oversight obligations give it freedom to make contextual adjustments, but it does not have the full benefit of external, objective professional feedback. Contextually, it is not formally committed to alignment with Spain's higher educational standards; it functions as a private religious institution.

Required collection of internal and external institutional feedback is another value of civil accreditation. External feedback includes graduates and employers who, in this context, represent the church. Feedback is a rich resource for guiding contextualization and holds potential for bearing the fruits of listening. The oversight of an accrediting or, in the case of seminary C, an external validating institution, compels the institutions to practice self-evaluation, to receive feedback from across the faith community, and to be accountable to the norms of like institutions within their contexts.

The Fruit of the Contextual Wisdom of the Church

Listening to the wisdom of local ecclesial communities can provide contextually relevant data about the three contexts served by seminaries: the institution, the church, and the society. A significant result of this research was the valuable survey data collected from church members. The five summative perspectives that emerged produced a series of implications for theological education in Madrid: theological and biblical knowledge are necessary components in the formation of ministry leaders; theological formation should be holistic and balanced, integrating experiential practice with knowledge; ministry leaders should be equipped to facilitate the development of a participatory community of believers; theological education should be accessible to everyone in the church; and the community of faith needs to remain theologically faithful as it engages and serves the non-confessing society. The challenge to the seminaries will be to establish a consistent practice of listening to gather qualitative data from the wider faith community, laity and clergy, that will inform the shaping of their designs and practices. For example, a simple annual survey could be distributed in churches or brief interviews conducted with representative laity, but these practices will need to be intentionally and regularly incorporated into institutional designs and practices.

Seminary students, who are often a demographically, denominationally, and ethnically diverse population, represent a particular source for communal wisdom for the seminaries. Students are like a bridge that connects the seminaries and the churches in a two-way flow of information. Going out from the seminaries, students share their seminary-acquired knowledge and skills with the faith community. Although some congregations may be wary of the new ideas and information that students bring, seminaries, informed of that contextual reality, can consider how to prepare students to respond to that type of reception and how they can address it with grace. Returning to the seminary, students bring reports and insights that offer a rich source of contextual data about their churches and the issues that the congregations are facing, both internally and externally, as they engage with the society. The student interview data in this research was thoughtful, specific, and contextually descriptive. Celucien L. Joseph writes, "Arguably, community knowledge and students' experiences are essential ingredients in the creation of the theological curriculum and to achieve an adequate, relevant, and contextualized theological education."[18] The practice of listening to the communal wisdom of all members of the church engages the seminary in a collaborative contextualization practice with the church.

The Fruit of Theological Discernment and Cultural Parables

The seminaries' embodied practices of hospitality emerged from the case study data as formative opportunities for contextualized engagement and theological formation. Café conversations are a Spanish ritual, a significant source of information for the careful listener, and an experience in cultural immersion that includes informal lessons on tradition, attitudes, customs, and values. The three contexts with which many seminaries engage—institution, church, and society—culturally intersect over coffee or a local beverage served when people meet together for conversation. Contextualization applies to the words, actions, methods, and frameworks that are used to communicate faith. The institutions can guide students through theological reflection on familiar cultural practices, such as café conversations, to discern the cultural-theological intersections that facilitate engagement between the church and society. Many of these cultural rituals are rich with theological significance.

18. Joseph, *Theological Education*, 13.

Seminary A provides economic hospitality to its students through the personal financial sacrifices of the faculty, who know that they are investing in the future of the church. Three of the faculty members of seminary B spoke of the ecumenical hospitality that they had received as students: one was welcomed as an evangelical conservative, another as a woman, and the third as a questioning scientist. Seminary C offers hospitality through its open enrollment policy and told the story of one of its graduates who was admitted into the program with no previous higher education. Through these familiar enculturated practices of hospitality characteristic of Spanish and/or of Christian community, the faculty contextually engage their students with theological lessons on generosity, sacrifice, hospitality, and love. Recognizing the theologically formative value in these well-established hospitable acts offers another opportunity to facilitate contextually responsive practices.

The institutional design can intentionally incorporate these parabolic rituals to both teach and model for students designs and practices that they can incorporate as they equip the people in the church to serve one another and to reach out to the people in their local communities. The intentional inclusion of theological formation through participation in these types of experiences and educational modalities will require modifications in the current curricular designs, a move away from the traditional classroom towards the type of practical and relational formation desired by both the students and survey participants. Jesus told parables, stories set in the life experiences of the local community to teach the people theological truths about life in the kingdom of God. Understanding and communicating the theological import of local cultural or ecclesial practices represents a fifth opportunity for contextualized educational formation.

Contextualization and Capacity for Adaptation

The disposition of an institution or church towards expanding the range of its contextualization practices relies on its capacity to adjust and adapt—characteristics that are incorporated, often unintentionally, into their designs. To determine capacity, one must examine the factors that can limit or restrict the types and extent of adjustments that can be made. Factors impacting the capacity for change include doctrine, resources, physical location, traditions, attitudes, policies, or external factors in the societal context. Societal factors can be political, legal, religious, sociological, geographic, or economic. Seminary A has less capacity. Its denominational and doctrinal commitments hold it to its original design. Although it has sacrificially met civil accreditation requirements, it holds firmly to its historic mission to equip men and women for ministry. Selecting content serves as its anchor, keeping it closely moored to its original design and practices. Seminary B has exhibited a significant capacity for adaptation in its multiple relocations, compliance with civil accreditation, transition to online delivery, and in its embrace of a new student demographic. The downside is that its denomination provides few students, and due to its commitment to ecumenism, the seminary is increasingly marginalized from the greater Protestant evangelical community. Seminary C would seem to have the greatest flexibility, with no building, no salaries, and a less formal relationship with its sponsoring institution. Yet, its minimalist design and low budget limits its ability to develop resources, sponsor lectureships, or extend its program and influence across Spain.

Intentionality is a significant component in contextual adaptation regardless of one's capacity for change. Purposeful change weighs the costs, plans the process, and safeguards faithfulness to institutional mission and identity. Faculty at seminaries A and B used the metaphor of swirling currents to illustrate the volatility of their present context. Neither being carried away nor simply going with the flow characterize a well-developed proactive capacity for contextual adaptation. Intentional navigation of these or any other swirling contexts can only happen if institutions, churches, or people theologically evaluate their current context, analyze their capacity for change, implement practices that facilitate contextualization, and finally, proactively adapt.

Contextualization and Spain's Protestant Evangelical Church

The three seminaries share a common challenge to theologically educate and empower Spain's theologically weak and resource-poor Protestant church. Although they have established relationships that facilitate their formational connection with the church, they continue to face contextualization challenges. The source of the church's weakness, perhaps surprisingly, does not lie in an absence or even lack of theological education and expertise within Spain. Although the seminaries are distinct from one another, each has highly qualified Spanish and international scholars and theologians. Faculty at all three seminaries minister as pastors, teachers, and members in local churches. They are personally and relationally present and engaged with the faith community, experiencing it from within even as they reflect on it from the vantage point of their institutions. All three seminaries have maintained their relational ties with their founding denominations. Each seminary utilizes several practices to disseminate theological education to churches. They invite ministry leaders and church members to their classes and workshops. They include denominational leaders on their seminary boards and committees. Faculty go to churches to preach and offer seminars, and they publish literature for the faith community.

However, the effectiveness of the seminaries' various methods of engagement with the church are hindered by a formidable, yet intangible obstacle: the church/academy divide. The faculty of all three seminaries referred to the existence of this suggested barrier between the academy and the church. Some churches exhibit a deeply ingrained defensive posture towards those who may think or believe differently than they do. It was noted that some value spiritually received knowledge over academic theological study. However, the parishioners who participated in the survey presented a contrasting characterization of the church as a community with a significant level of interest in theological education. This is good news that the seminaries can leverage as they continue to work to build trust with the church and mitigate the church's misconceptions about academic theological study.

Younger Generations

Two demographics were highlighted in the research data: the younger generations and Latin Americans, one ethnicity in Spain's increasingly diverse population. Spain's younger generations were described as hungry for education and knowledgeable about societal challenges and complexities. The historically educationally poor church is often ill-equipped to respond to this generation's searching questions about faith. The seminaries, however, function as ecclesial institutions of higher education and investigation. Seminaries B and C are poised to receive inquisitive seekers, one through its broad ecumenical reach and the other through its wide-open enrollment policy. However, accessibility has not produced significant increases in the number of students, and both seminaries experience challenges with student retention, issues that suggest the advisability of further contextual investigation into the mindset and culture of Spain's young adults.

Hunger for knowledge is only one characteristic of this demographic. Seminary A has identified two additional characteristics: a weakness in their character formation, evidenced by a lack of vocational clarity and maturity, and their relationship with money. Based on Rector A's statements, seminary A is not yet designed to accommodate those developmental needs for self-discovery; the faculty continue to reminisce about how students used to be, both in character and in their attitude towards money. Seminary A's residential campus, a potential nurturing seedbed, could be adapted to incorporate practices of character formation to serve this demographic. This is the historic practice of *paideia*. Student suggestions of mentorships and apprenticeships may be examples of communal wisdom that can facilitate adjustments in the design and practices to address this contextual reality.

Latin Americans

The relative absence of references in the interview data to the growing Latin American presence in Spain's Protestant evangelical churches merits consideration. It suggests that the institutions are delayed or nonreactive in their response to these developments. Indigenous Spaniards may now be only one of several ethnic groups in many congregations. Chloe T. Sun recently commented on the critical need for theological education to consider the implications of increasing demographic diversity: "Consequently, it is logical to anticipate a future of theological education marked by its global nature, with increasing diversity of cultural demographics within schools, more students from diasporic communities, an expanding number of educational models and a growing pluralism of theological practices."[19]

These institutions are confronted with the urgent and overdue necessity to teach and model cross-cultural analysis and communication, respect for and understanding of cultural differences, and community. Migration into and out of Spain has been constant since the 1980s with many migrants having sought refuge and community in Spain's evangelical churches. The current leadership in all three seminaries is primarily Spanish. To adapt these primarily indigenous seminaries to effectively equip students to serve in ethnically diverse settings will require adjustments to their current designs and practices. This could include hiring a more ethnically diverse faculty and staff, intentionally forming relationships with churches that have ethnically diverse congregations, and developing

---

19. Sun, *Great Things for God*, 6.

courses and training in intercultural and cross-cultural ministry for students serving in Spain as well as overseas.

Contextualization in the Context of the Society

The seminaries and the churches they serve operate in the wider context of Spain's complex society. As a collection of theological scholars, the seminaries have a responsibility to model faith and to theologically evaluate the messages and practices of the society as they provide leadership to the Protestant evangelical community that seeks to faithfully live out its faith. The research identified two indicative characteristics of an institution's capacity for contextual engagement with the society. The first is relational proximity, or an institution's presence (physical or digital) and approachability in relation to the society. Does the institution avoid or have only guarded contact with the non-confessing community? Or, does it seek connections through communication and the development of relationships? The second characteristic is inclusivity. With whom is the institution willing to partner, to consult, or admit as a student? These characteristics represent the distinction between open and fixed boundaries, both of which can be intentional theological practices to preserve an institution's faithfulness within the context of society.

Seminary A's residential environment and vocational mission currently exhibit minimal proximity and qualified inclusivity; accreditation requires inclusivity, but they are explicit about the confessional orientation and norms of their campus. Their residential community provides a safe, dedicated context for communal formation. Seminary B has ample digital proximity, accessible globally through the worldwide web, and ecumenical inclusivity, an inviting context for some yet intolerable for others who prefer to keep strict doctrinal boundaries. Seminary C's proximity is limited to seven Saturdays per year when classes meet, although they also have an online presence. They offer an open educational context where all who are interested can sample theological education without the pressure of having to be immersed in full-time study, but the level of engagement is severely limited by the infrequency of the class sessions.

A Theology of Work

An unexpected yet welcome discovery emerged out of the recurring student and survey participant references to the societal context of work. They are looking to the theological institutions to equip and support them with formation that enables them to faithfully engage as laborers in their local communities.[20] This is an example of the contextual wisdom within the Protestant faith community. This request, to be theologically equipped to live out their faith in their day-to-day lives, essentially challenges the seminaries to keep pace with society for the sake of the church. Seminaries and churches will need to adapt their designs and formational practices to equip people with the theological knowledge and skills to practice their faith in all contexts: the institution, the church, and the society.

Questions for Reflection

1. What are the advantages of having indigenous or locally experienced people contextualize design and instruction? How could their process be communicated to nonindigenous people to enable them to teach and communicate with contextual effectiveness? What are the advantages of having an outsider evaluate the contextualization process?
2. Which of the five contextualization practices is currently needed where you are serving? Give your reasons for that choice. If this list inspired you to think of an additional practice, describe it and how it will enhance your institution's relevance and engagement with students, the church, or society.
3. Describe your institution's capacity for contextualization.
4. Which people groups, or demographics, are not yet being fully included or served by your institution? What adjustments or additions in your institutional design and practices will be needed to serve those people?
5. How is your institution engaging with society? How would or is a robust theology of work facilitating the outreach of the church in the community?

---

20. Greene, "The Great Divide." This article was my introduction into the theology of work.

7

Conclusion: Planting Seeds

It is a critical time in which to converse about our challenges, to strategize about how to tackle the changing landscape in theological education, and to move forward with hope.

—CHLOE T. SUN[1]

FRUIT HAS WITHIN ITSELF the potential to bear more fruit through its seeds. This chapter presents a summation of salient discoveries grounded in the breadth of the research, potential "seeds" that others may take away and plant in their own distinctive contexts. First, a list of six contextually situated "shaping powers" offers a valid and extendible framework for seminaries functioning in a variety of global contexts to utilize as they evaluate the contextual effectiveness of institutional designs and practices. Next, it highlights some of the research's original contributions to knowledge, possible resources that could be adapted by others in their contextualization efforts. The results are particularly relevant for institutions that may have begun with imported designs and practices or that serve minority faith populations in resource poor contexts. Finally, it gives suggestions for further investigation, a potential harvest of new fruit.

---

1. Sun, *Great Things for God*, 150.

Six "Shaping Powers"

The Shaping Power of Our Institutional Heritage

First, it is important to recognize the shaping power of our institutional heritage and theological traditions on institutional designs and practices. The four continua offer a simple, transferrable, and adaptable framework that can be applied to determine and evaluate the underlying philosophies, presuppositions, and embedded traditions shaping many of our institutional aims, the population we seek to serve, the educational methodologies we implement, and our location in relation to the church and society. Understanding the influential impact of our history equips institutions with a new vantage point from which they can make informed decisions about what designs and practices they believe should be maintained, contextualized, or released as they anticipate both present and future needs of the church and society.

The Shaping Power of Our Historical and Current Cultural Context

Second, the identification and understanding of the shaping forces at work within our local or national historical and present cultural context is critical for thorough, knowledgeable adjustments. Developing a habit of theological attentiveness as both a design feature and a practice can identify "power interests" and "root metaphors" that may be clouding institutional objectivity and hindering our ability to dream and contextualize.[2] The implementation of critical remembering, ethnographic research, or practical theological reflection can facilitate the adaptation of a seminary's designs and practices. Modeling these practices will equip students with skills to do likewise as they lead the communities they serve towards relevant contextually responsive change.

The Shaping Power of Communal Wisdom

Third, the communal wisdom of the church—laity, clergy, scholars, and students—holds creative potential to shape theological education through the multifaceted range of perspectives it can provide. Everyone in the church

---

2. Vanhoozer, "Everyday Theology," 50–52.

is a recipient of theological education, some directly through intentional study and others indirectly as they engage in or respond to the teaching and practices of the church. Listening to people from across this community invites them to collaborate in theological formation; it is an expression of inclusion and facilitates accessibility to theological education. The collective of perspectives and experiences from across the entire faith community can provide seminaries with broad spectrum feedback on the effectiveness of its graduates, insights into the parishioners' expectations of what to expect in and from their ministry leaders, information on church and societal issues, and parishioners' attitudes towards theological formation. Current designs and practices can be evaluated based on the fruits of listening to ensure that contextualized adaptations will facilitate the training of ministry leaders to equip them to serve in local communities.

The Shaping Power of Demographic Shifts

Fourth, demographic shifts in the communities where theological institutions are located or where their students will be serving call for contextually appropriate adaptation of curricula, forms of communication, and awareness of changing cultural and social dynamics and their implications for theological formation and ministry. The theological institution can serve as a model for the faith community of how to welcome, adapt, and serve in intercultural and cross-cultural contexts.

The Shaping Power of Academic Accreditation

Fifth, formal relationships with educational accrediting organizations that function within the same cultural and societal context can provide expertise, oversight, and recognition for theological institutions. These agencies direct seminaries in contextual adaptations of their designs and practices to bring them into conformity with standards of higher education. Although the requirements are demanding, such as the development of student competencies, required collection of feedback, and organizational transparency, they offer theological education institutions tools for contextualized revisions and accountability for the continued effectiveness and professionalism of their designs and practices.

The Shaping Power of Outward-Focused Theological Reflection

Sixth, the knowledge and discernment of theological educators can provide guidance and leadership to the church in how to respond and engage with changing norms and practices in society. Theological educators may tend to postpone cultural hermeneutical theological reflection in order to address the immediate inward-focused needs of the institution and church. However, this research found that the church is looking to the institutions to equip them to serve and work in society with integrity, eloquence, and compassion. Theologically navigating societal "swirling currents," as they have been described in the data, calls theological educators to fulfil a prophetic leadership role for the church and informs their selection on the type of formation that students may need in order to equip the church in faithful living and witness.

Originality and Contribution to Knowledge

This research has introduced several tools that can be applied in the analysis of an institution's design and practices. The five contextualization practices and the implications of the survey participants' perspectives are resources that can be utilized as institutions or churches evaluate the effectiveness of their designs and practices. Another tool is the model of four continua, adapted from Goodbourn's work, that can facilitate the contextual analysis of a theological institution's educational priorities. This tool can be used to graphically represent four foci: an institution's aim, its intended students, its educational methodologies, and its location in relation to the church and society.

The practice of critical remembering, another tool, applied to the historical experiences of Spain's Protestants and in the analysis of the seminary case studies uncovered contextual themes in the evangelical community: scarcity, fragility, minority status, and the desire for legitimacy. By identifying these themes, this research offers Spain's Protestant evangelical seminaries and churches a resource for reflection and an opportunity to critically re-remember and possibly reinterpret these experiences in the light of their present knowledge, experiences, and faith. The practice of critical remembering can be utilized by seminaries, churches, and communities to explore, analyze, and respond to the shaping power of the past on the present.

The survey "Perspectives on Theological Education" collected qualitative data that revealed the perspectives and experiences of Madrid's Protestant faith community. The rich data contributed by the respondents is not only original, but it validates the importance of listening to the laity's perspectives on theological education. The survey tool is included in appendix 2.

Situating the research in the Protestant community of Spain brings this minority population and its history into the awareness of the global church. Spain was re-evangelized in the 1800s by Protestant missionaries and, like many nations in the Global South, evangelized at that time. Spain's Protestant church shares similar contextualization struggles in its appropriation of some imported aspects of their faith practices. Because it is a European country, this reality has often gone unobserved.

Suggestions for Future Research

The outcomes of this research suggest several areas for further investigation. The ministry model of *acompañamiento* (to accompany, or as expressed in the survey, to work and walk alongside of parishioners) should be further developed for the purpose of designing a curriculum to facilitate the formation of ministry practitioners with relational team-building abilities. Local societal issues need to be identified with the assistance of communal wisdom. Listening to the local faith community is an important, available, and inexpensive resource that theological institutions can utilize to determine whether they are equipping students with the theological understanding and skills to support and theologically empower the church. Considering trends in global migration, theological education should incorporate multiethnic responsive designs and practices—for example, training in cross-cultural communication, language acquisition, peacemaking, an ethical response to immigration, or the development of a theology of the sojourner or stranger. Theological institutions can serve as a model for local churches ministering in increasingly ethnically diverse contexts.

Conclusion

This research harvested the fruits of listening. A survey was developed to give people who attend local churches an opportunity to share their perspectives on theological education. They expressed their desire for accessible theological formation that equips leaders to relationally empower the church. Each seminary presented a distinctive design and approach to formation, as per the continua. The legacies that they have inherited from centuries of theological education continue to root them in the historic practices of theological formation. All three institutions voiced narratives of how they must find ways to persevere amid pervasive scarcity, a fragile church, and a rapidly changing society. Their stories prompted further research into the history of Spain's Protestant community, which enriched and informed the discovery of the distinctive "root metaphors" that continue to impact their perspectives.[3] The culminating results produced five contextualization practices, the fruits of listening: critical remembering, theological reflection that keeps pace with society, accreditation as contextual engagement, listening to the contextual wisdom of the church, and the theological discernment of cultural parables.

---

3. Vanhoozer, "Everyday Theology," 52.

APPENDIX 1
The Fruits of Listening
Five Contextualization Practices

CRITICAL REMEMBERING: CRITICAL REMEMBERING explores and analyzes how experiences and memories of the past continue to influence actions and beliefs in the present. The aim is to theologically evaluate the relevance and truth of that influence with reference to the realities of the present context and the faithfulness of God and to move forward in that knowledge.

Theological reflection that keeps pace with society: The complex and dynamic context of society requires the fearless exercise of theological discernment to interpret and evaluate the messages and actions of the world. The aim is to preserve faithfulness to Christ in how the church speaks and engages the world with boldness and love.

Accreditation as contextual engagement: Academic alignment with accrediting organizations leverages the value of their expertise and requires contextualization of an institution's designs and practices to the established norms. The aim is to open doors to greater institutional excellence, provide increased educational opportunities for students, and to strengthen the legitimacy of the seminary in its role in the community.

Listening to the contextual wisdom of the church: Inviting members from across the community of faith to contribute insights, experiences, and needs can produce a body of profound, multifaceted wisdom for theological education and the church. The aim is to facilitate greater engagement and strengthen relationships among the institution, the church, and the society.

Theological discernment of cultural parables: The discernment of the theological implications embedded in cultural and routine practices provides seminaries with a range of familiar experiences that can be intentionally incorporated into their instruction to contextualize and apply the teachings of Scripture. The aim is to equip the church with cultural parables to communicate the story of Christ through images, experiences, and stories set within the local society.

APPENDIX 2

Survey

Perspectives on Theological Education

Section 1 of 6

YOU ARE BEING INVITED to take part in a research survey. Before you decide whether or not to take part, it is important for you to understand why the research is being done and what it will involve. Please take time to read the following information carefully.

The aims of this survey are: (1) To give you the opportunity to share your perspectives and ideas about theological education. Generally, this is education for people working in church leadership as well as for people who want to know more about God. (2) To identify possible factors that may have contributed to the formation of your perspectives. Your responses are important and valuable. Whether you have had much experience with theological education or not, I am interested in knowing your perspectives on theological education.

These surveys are being distributed in various evangelical Christian churches in the province of Madrid. The leadership of your church has given permission to distribute this survey to those who attend the church. Your participation is totally voluntary.

This survey is anonymous. None of the questions asks for personally identifiable information. Paper copies of the survey will be collected after completion for the purpose of analysis and comparison during the research process. The online surveys will pass through the same analysis and comparison. Paper copies of the surveys will be destroyed upon completion of the written research report. If you or your organization would like to receive a report of the final statistical results and analysis, please contact me at this email address: cfitch@nazarene.ac.uk.

It is my hope that this information will assist those involved in theological education to serve you, the community of believers, with greater understanding and relevance. I am conducting this research as a part of my doctoral research program at Nazarene Theological College and the University of Manchester. The survey and the data collection process have been approved by the Research Ethics Committee. I served in theological education and church ministry in Madrid for nearly fifteen years. This project represents my desire to support the ministry of evangelical Christian churches in Spain as well as in other areas of the world.

If you have any concerns about the process or manner in which this study has been conducted, please contact the chair of the Research Ethics Committee via enquiries@nazarene.ac.uk.

Completion of this survey indicates that you have consented to participate.

—Colleen Fitch

Section 2 of 6

Introduction to Survey

This survey asks about your thoughts, opinions, and experiences. Sections 3 and 6 formulate general questions about your situation and experiences in relation to theological education. Sections 4–5, propose questions about your opinions regarding theological education and its purpose. Simply click on the button "NEXT" to continue to the next section until the end of the survey. Although you can skip questions, it would be good to try and answer all of them unless a question does not pertain to you. The entire survey takes about 10–15 minutes to complete.

Thank you for your willingness to participate and to assist in this research project.

To complete the survey, it is necessary to confirm that you are eighteen years or older and give your consent to participate: Yes or No.

Section 3 of 6

General Information

This general information will be used to anonymously describe the population taking this survey.

1. Select your current age range from the list. The choices include: 18–24 years old; 25–34 years old; 35–50 years old; 51–65 years old; 66–80 years old; 81 or more.
2. Gender. Choices include: Female, Male.
3. Nationality. The choices include: Spanish, Other.
4. If you are not from Spain, which is the geographic region of your nationality? The choices include: Europe; Central and Eastern Asia; Middle East; Australia and Pacific Islands; Africa; South America; Central America; North America.
5. Which best represents your family faith background? Please select no more than two. The choices include: Roman Catholic; Christian Evangelical; Muslim; Jewish; Eastern Religion; Atheist/Agnostic; Other.
6. What is the approximate length of time that you have attended an evangelical church? The choices include: Less than 1 year; 1–5 years; 6–10 years; 11–25 years; more than 26 years.
7. In which church sponsored activities do you participate? Check all that apply. Choices include: Prayer meeting; Worship service; Sunday school; Mid-week Bible study or fellowship group; Community service; Church administration; Other.
8. Which title best describes your current involvement in your church? Choose all that apply. Choices include: Pastor; Teacher; Worship/Musician; Finance; Member; Visitor; Other.
9. Which category best describes your church? Mark only one. Choices include: Anglican; Reformed, IEE, and Presbyterian; Baptist and Free Church (FIEDE); Assembly of Brethren; Pentecostal; Church of Philadelphia; Charismatic; Nazarene, Mennonite, Free Methodist, Church of Christ, or Christian Missionary Alliance; Evangelical or Interdenominational Churches; Adventist.

APPENDIX 2: SURVEY

Section 4 of 6

Your thoughts about the relationship of theological education to the church and the society

10. A university degree is valued by the people in the society where you live. A four-point Likert scale ranging from Strongly Disagree to Strongly Agree.
11. The primary purpose of seminaries or biblical institutions is to serve and support the church. Four-point Likert scale ranging from Strongly Disagree to Strongly Agree.
12. Pastors and church leaders need specialized education and training to be in ministry. Four-point Likert scale ranging from Strongly Disagree to Strongly Agree.
13. Theological and biblical training prepares people to communicate the Christian faith to the local society. Four-point Likert scale ranging from Strongly Disagree to Strongly Agree.
14. Practical "hands-on" experience is more important than academic study for those called to be pastors and ministry leaders. Four-point Likert scale ranging from Strongly Disagree to Strongly Agree.
15. Theological education should equip people to serve the needs of the community and to address issues of social justice. Four-point Likert scale ranging from Strongly Disagree to Strongly Agree.
16. Theological education equips people with knowledge and experience to practice their faith. Four-point Likert scale ranging from Strongly Disagree to Strongly Agree.
17. Foreigners, such as missionaries, are the ones who have usually established centers for theological education. Four-point Likert scale ranging from Strongly Disagree to Strongly Agree.
18. Knowing how to think theologically is helpful for making routine daily decisions. Four-point Likert scale ranging from Strongly Disagree to Strongly Agree.

In your opinion, what degree of importance do these qualities and skills have for effective leadership? The following list of qualities are each rated on a four-point Likert scale from Not important to Very important.

19. To be equipped by the Spirit
20. To have theological and biblical knowledge
21. To be able to preach dynamically
22. To have moral integrity
23. To know how to train new leaders
24. To have administrative abilities
25. To provide pastoral care
26. To be involved in social justice affairs
27. To be committed to evangelism and missions
28. To be self-assured
29. To be a leader with vision
30. To be flexible
31. To have the ability to work with all ages
32. Write down any abilities or qualities that are missing from the list. Open response.

Section 5 of 6

Your understanding of the phrase "theological education"

What does it mean? Who is it for? What activities does it include?

33. In your opinion, what is the most important purpose/goal of theological education? Mark only one oval. The choices include: The development of spiritual maturity; The development of practical skills for ministry; The development of theological and biblical understanding.
34. In your opinion, for whom is formal theological education necessary? Mark only one oval. The choices include: It is necessary for people called to be pastors, teachers, missionaries or Christian leaders; It is necessary for all Christians; It is not necessary, but some people

APPENDIX 2: SURVEY

could benefit from or enjoy theological studies; It is not necessary for anyone.

35. In your opinion, the most effective setting for theological education is? Mark only one. The choices include: A solitary and quiet place; A seminary or Bible institute; A church; A center for spiritual formation; Anywhere.

In your opinion, what types of formation should be facilitated by theological education? The following list of types of formation are each rated on a four-point Likert scale from Not important to Very important.

36. Formation in personal spirituality
37. Formation in leadership
38. Formation in biblical and theological knowledge
39. Formation in the practice of reflecting theologically about life and society
40. Formation as a lifelong learner
41. Formation in personal integrity
42. Write down any type of formation that is missing in the list. Open response.

What abilities or practices should be developed in/during theological education? The following list of abilities are each rated on a four-point Likert scale from Not important to Very important.

43. Ability to practice spiritual disciplines like prayer and fasting
44. Ability to teach
45. Ability to equip and train others
46. Ability to preach
47. Ability to administrate or lead/direct
48. Ability to minister to children and youth
49. Ability to evangelize
50. Ability to serve the local community
51. Ability to provide pastoral care
52. Ability to practice theological reflection in every aspect of life

53. Write down any abilities or practices that are missing in the list. Open response.

Classify the importance of these courses for equipping a person to carry out Christian ministry or to be a pastor of a church. The following list of types of formation are each rated on a four-point Likert scale from Not important to Very important.

54. Church History
55. History of the Reformation
56. New Testament
57. Old Testament
58. Biblical Languages: Greek and Hebrew
59. Theology and Doctrine
60. The Trinity: Father, Son, and Holy Spirit
61. Eschatology: The Study of the "End Times"
62. Spiritual Warfare
63. Christian Ethics
64. Social Justice
65. Apologetics: How to Defend the Faith
66. Science and Faith
67. General Philosophy
68. The Preaching of Sermons
69. Pastoral Care
70. Church Administration
71. Worship
72. Methods for Effective Teaching
73. Marriage and Family
74. Youth Ministry
75. Evangelism and Missions
76. Church Planting
77. World Religions

APPENDIX 2: SURVEY

78. Spiritual Formation: Prayer, Fasting, Etc.
79. What courses are missing in the list? Open response.

Section 6 of 6

Your contact with theological education

This is the final section. Please click on the SUBMIT tab when you are finished.

80. How are people equipped for leadership and ministry in your church? Open response.
81. What or who best helps you to learn how to follow Christ in today's society? Open response.
82. Has the pastor of your church studied in a seminary or Bible institute? Choices include: Yes; No; Do not know.
83. How many people do you know who have taken classes at a Bible institute or seminary. The choices include: 0; 1; 2–4; 5–10; 11 or more.
84. Professors who teach at Bible institutes or seminaries speak or teach in your church. . . . The choices include: Every week; Several times during the year; Once a year; Never.
85. Is there information posted in your church that advertises study programs in a seminary or Bible institute? Choices include: Yes; No; Do not know.
86. Does your church support or send students to a particular seminary or Bible institute? The choices include: Yes; No; Do not know.
87. If you answered "yes," where is that seminary or Bible institute located in relationship to your church? The choices include: Within the very church; In the province of Madrid; In a different province in Spain; In a different country; Online.
88. How does that seminary or Bible institute serve your church? Open response.
89. Have you visited the web page of a seminary or Bible institute? The choices include: Yes; No.

90. Have you physically visited a Bible institute or seminary? Choices include: Yes; No.
91. Have you taken any courses in a Bible institute or seminary? Choices include: Yes; No.
92. If you answered "yes" to having taken one or more courses, did you complete a degree or receive a certificate from that institute or seminary? Choices include: Yes; No.
93. What degree or certificate did you receive? Open response.
94. If you have taken courses at a Bible institute or theological seminary, how do those studies contribute to your life and practice of faith? Open response.
95. Do you think there are comments or observations about theological education that would be important to include in this survey? Please share them here: Open response.

Thank you!

APPENDIX 3
Faculty Interview Questions

1. What is your role in this institution, and how did you become involved in it?
2. What is the vision and mission statement of this institution?
3. In what ways has it been developed to provide education and training contextually designed for Spain?
4. What are the greatest challenges or obstacles that you face?
5. When and how was the course of study selected and designed? How often do you evaluate its effectiveness? Who has the authority to decide or to make the changes? What factors have the most weight in those evaluations?
6. How does this institution uniquely serve the evangelical community of Spain?
7. Are there unique Spanish contextual theological, social, or church concerns that you need to address?
8. Let's talk about the potential influence of several external groups; what impact do they have on what is included in the course of study?
    - An independent board
    - Denominational affiliation
    - Local pastors and/or church leaders
    - Students

- Accreditation or other governmental requirements
- Other

9. How does the institution relate to or serve the local church? Are the faculty encouraged or expected to be serving in some type of ministry in addition to teaching?
10. Tell me a story of when you've seen how this institution is making a positive impact in how the church is engaging in mission here in Spain?
11. Is there anything that you would like to add or that you think has been left out of this discussion?[1]

---

1. Krueger and Casey, *Focus Groups*, 43–46.

APPENDIX 4

Student Interview Questions

1. What are you studying, and what motivated you to choose this course of studies?
2. How have your studies and experiences at this institution changed the way you think or act?
3. Considering the cultural history of Spain and as well as the current social climate, what types of formation would be particularly helpful or important for you to be equipped to serve any unique needs or characteristics of the Spanish evangelical church? What types of formation are helpful or needed to effectively serve and communicate with the people in Spanish society, those outside the church?
4. Are there any courses or additional training that you would like to see included in the course of study? How would those courses be beneficial to you? Do any of the courses in the current curriculum seem to be more suited to a different context . . . maybe for America, South America, or other? Are the course materials generally up-to-date and relevant? What would you remove from the current course of study to make room for those new courses?
5. How do you relate to or serve in your local church?

6. What challenges or obstacles do you face in your studies or ministry?

    How about in relation to:
    - Your family?
    - Your church?
    - Your future?
    - Spanish society?

7. How is the institution equipping you to face those challenges?
8. Is there anything that you would like to add or that you think has been left out of this discussion?[1]

---

1. Kruger and Casey, *Focus Groups*, 43–46.

Bibliography

Aleshire, Daniel O. *Earthen Vessels: Hopeful Reflections on the Work and Future of Theological Schools.* Grand Rapids: Eerdmans, 2008. Kindle.
———. "The Future Has Arrived: Changing Theological Education in a Changed World." *Theological Education* 46.2 (2011) 69–80. https://www.ats.edu/files/galleries/2011-theological-education-v46-n2.pdf.
Álvarez Álvelo, Máximo. "España: Cronología 2019; Incremento de Iglesias Evangélicas." Edited by Javier Vázquez Artero. Sevilla: Evangelismo Al Fondo, 2019. https://estaticos.qdq.com/swdata/files/702/702528463/ESPANA-IGLESIAS-2019_weHcXqV.pdf.
———. "Estadística Total España: 1993–2019." Edited by Javier Vázquez Artero. Sevilla: Evangelismo a Fondo, 2019. https://estaticos.qdq.com/swdata/files/702/702528463/ESTADISTICA-TOTAL-ESPANA-1993---2019.pdf.
ANECA. "Informe de autoevaluación." Apr. 17, 2017. https://www.fliedner.es/media/modules/editor/seut/docs/informe-autoevaluacion-aneca-SEUT-2017.pdf.
"ANECA: Agencia Nacional de Evaluación de la Calidad y Acreditación." https://www.aneca.es/aneca.
Astor, Avi, et al. "The Politics of Religious Heritage: Framing Claims to Religion as Culture in Spain." *Journal for the Scientific Study of Religion* 56.1 (Mar. 2017) 126–42. https://doi.org/10.1111/jssr.12321.
Babbie, Earl. *Survey Research Methods.* 2nd ed. Belmont, CA: Wadsworth, 1990.
Banks, Robert. *Reenvisioning Theological Education: Exploring a Missional Alternative to Current Models.* Grand Rapids: Eerdmans, 1999.
Bergmann, Sigurd, and Mika Vähkängas. "Doing Situated Theology: Introductory Remarks about the History, Method, and Diversity of Contextual Theology." In *Contextual Theology: Skills and Practices of Liberating Faith,* edited by Sigurd Bergmann and Mika Vähkängas, 1–14. Routledge New Critical Thinking in Religion, Theology and Biblical Studies. New York: Routledge, 2021. Kindle.
Bevans, Stephen B. *Models of Contextual Theology.* Rev. ed. Faith and Culture Series. Maryknoll, NY: Orbis, 2002.

Bienenberg Center de Formation. "FBSE: Guide de l'etudiant(e) 2020-2021; Approfondir la foi et être équipé." https://static1.squarespace.com/static/5893052 9f7e0aba7b72289b2/t/5f8979b97219cf2a9dba88de/1602845155447/FBSE+Guide+de+l%27e%CC%81tudiant+2020-2021_v2.pdf.

"Bienvenido del decano." SEUT Facultad de Teología. https://www.facultadseut.org/es/bienvenida-decano-seut.

Brinkhoff, Thomas. "Alcobendas in Madrid (Madrid)." City Population, last modified Dec. 27, 2019. https://www.citypopulation.de/en/spain/madrid/madrid/28006__alcobendas/.

Browning, Don S. *A Fundamental Practical Theology: Descriptive and Strategic Proposals.* Minneapolis: Fortress, 1996.

Calahan, Kathleen A. "Three Approaches to Practical Theology, Theological Education, and the Church's Ministry." *International Journal of Practical Theology* 9.1 (July 2005) 63–94. https://www.librarysearch.manchester.ac.uk/permalink/44MAN_INST/1rfd42k/cdi_crossref_primary_10_1515_IJPT_2005_005.

Cameron, Helen, et al. *Talking about God in Practice: Theological Action Research and Practical Theology.* London: SCM, 2010.

Cannell, Linda. *Theological Education Matters: Leadership Education for the Church.* Newburgh, IN: EDCOT, 2008.

Carlos, Juan, I. "Ley 24/1992, de 10 de noviembre, por la que se aprueba el Acuerdo de Cooperación del Estado con la Federación de Entidades Religiosas Evangélicas de España." *Boletín Oficial del Estado* 272, Nov. 12, 1992. https://www.boe.es/eli/es/l/1992/11/10/24.

Casanova, Julián. *The Spanish Republic and Civil War.* Cambridge: Cambridge University Press, 2010. https://doi.org/10.1017/CBO9780511763137.

Centro de Investigaciones Sociológicas. "Barómetro de diciembre 2017." CIS 3199. Spain, 2017. https://www.cis.es/documents/d/cis/es3199marpdf.

———. "Barómetro de diciembre 2019: Postelectoral elecciones generales 2019; Distribuciones Marginales." CIS 3269. Spain, 2019. https://www.cis.es/documents/d/cis/es3269marpdf.

———. "Barómetro de diciembre: Expectativas 1998." CIS 2274. Spain, 1997. https://www.cis.es/documents/d/cis/Es2271pdf.

———. "Barómetro de febrero 1993: Desigualdad." CIS 2046. Spain, 1993. https://www.cis.es/documents/d/cis/es2046marpdf.

———. "Distribuciones marginales: Barómetro diciembre." CIS 2972. Spain, 2012. https://www.cis.es/documents/d/cis/Es2972pdf.

———. "Funciones." CIS. https://www.cis.es/el-cis/funciones. https://www.cis.es/documents/d/cis/es3194marpdf.

———. "Redes Sociales (I)/Religión (III) (ISSP)." CIS 3194. Spain, 2017. https://www.cis.es/documents/d/cis/es3194marpdf.

———. "Religión (II) ISSP." CIS 2776. Spain, 2008. https://www.cis.es/documents/d/cis/es2776pdf.

———. "Religión (International Social Survey Program): Ficha técnica." CIS 2301. Spain, 1998. https://www.cis.es/documents/d/cis/Es2301marpdf.

"Centro Teológico Kénosis." *El Mensajero* 101 (June 2011). https://www.menonitas.org/el_mensajero/2011/101/index.html.

Centro Teológico Koinonía. "Cursos del año 2023-2024." https://www.ceteka.org/course/index.php?categoryid=21.

———. "Cursos del año 2024–2025." https://www.ceteka.org/mod/page/view.php?id=1810.

———. *SWOT*. Madrid: OMS Theological Education, 2018.

"Centro Teológico Koinonía (CTK)." CTK, Aug. 6, 2012. YouTube, 1:27. https://www.youtube.com/watch?v=UHcfbNFgG5E.

Cheesman, Graham. "Competing Paradigms in Theological Education Today." *Evangelical Review of Theology* 17.4 (1993) 58–69. https://theology.worldea.org/wp-content/uploads/2020/12/ERT-17-4.pdf.

"Círculo de amigos de la facultad de teología SEUT." SEUT Facultad de Teología. https://www.facultadseut.org/es/informacion-general-patrocinio.

"Concluye el primer curso en CTK." *Protestante Digital*, May 28, 2012. https://www.protestantedigital.com/ciudades/27508/concluye-el-primer-curso-en-ctk.

Cosden, Darrell, and Donald Fairbairn. "Contextual Theological Education among Post-Soviet Protestants, Case Study 2: The Masters of Arts in Contextual Theology at Donetsk Christian University." *Transformation* 18.2 (April 2001) 125–36. https://journals.sagepub.com/doi/10.1177/026537880101800207.

Costas, Orlando E. "Theological Education and Mission." In *New Alternatives in Theological Education*, edited by C. René Padilla, 5–24. Oxford: Regnum, 1988.

Das, Rupen. *Connecting Curriculum with Context: A Handbook for Context Relevant Curriculum Development in Theological Education*. ICETE Series. Carlisle, UK: Langham Global Library, 2015. Kindle.

———. "Relevance and Faithfulness: Challenges in Contextualizing Theological Education." *Insights Journal for Global Theological Education* 1.2 (May 2016) 17–29. https://insightsjournal.org/relevance-and-faithfulness-challenges-in-contextualizing-theological-education/.

Díaz, Julio. "40 Años de Seminario Bautista en Alcobendas." *Protestante Digital*, Dec. 14, 2016. https://www.protestantedigital.com/ciudades/41008/40-anos-de-seminario-bautista-en-alcobendas.

"Diploma en estudios teológicos." UEBE Facultad de Teología. https://ftuebe.es/diploma-en-estudios-teologicos/.

Dockery, David S. "Theological Education: An Introduction." In *Theology, Church and Ministry: A Handbook for Theological Education*, edited by David S. Dockery, 3–22. Nashville: B&H Academic, 2017. Kindle.

Dowson, Martin, and Dennis M. McInerney. "For What Should Theological Colleges Educate? A Systematic Investigation of Ministry Education Perceptions and Priorities." *Review of Religious Research* 46.4 (June 2005) 403–21. https://www.jstor.org/stable/3512169.

Drelichman, Mauricio, et al. "The Long-Run Effects of Religious Persecution: Evidence from the Spanish Inquisition." *Proceedings of the National Academy of Sciences* 118.33 (2021) 1–9. https://doi.org/10.1073/pnas.2022881118.

Dykstra, Craig. "Reconceiving Practice." In *Shifting Boundaries: Contextual Approaches to the Structure of Theological Education*, edited by Barbara G. Wheeler and Edward Farley, 35–66. Louisville: Westminster John Knox, 1991.

Dykstra, Craig, and Dorothy C. Bass. "Times of Yearning, Practices of Faith." In *Practicing Our Faith: A Way of Life for a Searching People*, edited by Dorothy C. Bass, 1–12. The Practices of Faith Series. Minneapolis: Fortress, 2019. Kindle.

Edgar, Brian. "The Theology of Theological Education." *Evangelical Review of Theology* 29.3 (July 2005) 208–17. https://theology.worldea.org/wp-content/uploads/2020/12/ERT-29-3.pdf.

Escobar, Samuel. "La educación teológica y vocación pastoral." *Alétheia: Revista Evangélica de Teología* 46 (Feb. 2014) 19–36.
Espinoza, Benjamin D. "'Pia Desideria' Reimagined for Contemporary Theological Education." *The Asbury Journal* 70.1 (2015) 140–56. https://place.asburyseminary.edu/cgi/viewcontent.cgi?article=1299&context=asburyjournal.
Estruch, Juan. "How Can There Be Protestants in Spain?" *The Ecumenical Review* 20.1 (Jan. 1968) 53–62. https://onlinelibrary.wiley.com/doi/10.1111/j.1758-6623.1968.tb02188.x.
Faber, Sebastian. *Exhuming Franco: Spain's Second Transition.* Nashville: Vanderbilt University Press, 2021. Kindle.
Farley, Edward. *The Fragility of Knowledge: Theological Education in the Church and the University.* Philadelphia: Fortress, 1988.
———. *Theologia: The Fragmentation and Unity of Theological Education.* Eugene, OR: Wipf & Stock, 2001.
Feenstra, Ramon. "La reivindicación de la ética in la política: un análisis del movimiento de indignados." *Ometeca* 18.13 (2013) 13–29. http://hdl.handle.net/10234/114723.
FEREDE. "Caso pastores jubilados sin pensión: FEREDE considera la respuesta del Gobierno a la Comisión Europea de Derechos Humanos una 'maniobra dilatoria.'" *Actualidad Evangélica,* July 25, 2014. https://www.actualidadevangelica.es/index.php?option=com_content&view=article&id=7942%3Acaso-pastores-jubilados-sin-pension-ferede-considera-la-respuesta-del-gobierno-a-la-comision-europea-de-derechos-humanos-una-maniobra-dilatoria&catid=42%3Aferede&Itemid=209.
———. "Manifiesto por la libertad religiosa en España." Oct. 2011. https://www.actualidadevangelica.es/2011/pdf/Manifiesto-Libertad-Religiosa-Espana-2011.pdf.
———. *Vademécum Evangélico: 2017.* Madrid, 2017.
Ferenczi, Jason. *Serving Communities: Governance and the Potential of Theological Schools.* ICETE Series. Carlisle, UK: Langham Global Library, 2015.
Fernández, Enrique. "Engaging Contextual Realities in Theological Education: Systems and Strategies." *Evangelical Review of Theology* 38.4 (October 2014) 339–49. https://theology.worldea.org/wp-content/uploads/2020/12/ERT-38-4.pdf.
"El Gobierno español aprueba el RD que reconoce los efectos civiles de los títulos de teología protestantes." *Actualidad Evangélica,* Nov. 11, 2011. https://actualidadevangelica.es/index.php?option=com_content&view=article&id=3348:ultima-hora-el-gobierno-espanol-aprueba-el-rd-que-reconoce-los-efectos-civiles-de-los-titulos-de-teologia-Protestantes&catid=46:actualidad.
González, Justo L. *The History of Theological Education.* Nashville: Abingdon, 2015.
González Fernández, Antonio. "Anabaptist Theology Formation Centre (CTK)." Mennonite Central Committee (MCC) Report. Madrid: MCC, July 10, 2014.
———. "Cinco años de CTK." *El Mensajero* 156 (June–July 2016). https://www.menonitas.org/el_mensajero/2016/156/03.html.
———. "El desafío de una Teología Evangélica en España." *Carthaginensia: Revista de Estudios e Investigación* 34.66 (July–Dec. 2018) 435–48. https://revistacarthaginensia.com/index.php/CARTHAGINENSIA/article/view/12.
González Fernández, Antonio, and Sergio Rosell. "El cristianismo tiene mucho que decir en nuestro tiempo." Interview by Pedro Tarquis. *Protestante Digital,* Sept. 5, 2012. Vimeo, 19:31. https://vimeo.com/48897086.
———. "CTK: Centro Teológico Kenosis." Interview by Pedro Tarquis. *Protestante Digital,* Sept. 12, 2012. Vimeo, 20:26. https://vimeo.com/49317721.

Goodbourn, David. "Mapping Church-Related Adult Education." *British Journal of Theological Education* 11.2 (2001) 39–47. https://doi.org/10.1558/jate.v11i2.39.

"Grado en teología." UEBE Facultad de Teología. https://ftuebe.es/grado-en-teologia/.

Graham, Elaine, et al. *Theological Reflection: Methods*. 4th ed. London: SCM, 2010.

Graham, Helen. *The Spanish Civil War: A Very Short Introduction*. Oxford: Oxford University Press, 2005. Kindle.

Greene, Mark. "The Great Divide: Mark Greene on the Biggest Challenge Facing the Church Today . . . and What We Can Do about It." London: LICC, 2010. https://licc.org.uk/wp-content/uploads/2017/03/The-Great-Divide-Mark-Greene-1.pdf.

Hauerwas, Stanley. *The Work of Theology*. Grand Rapids: Eerdmans, 2015.

"Historia de la Fundación Federico Fliedner." Fundación Federico Fliedner. https://www.fliedner.es/es/historia.

Hough, Joseph C., Jr., and John B. Cobb Jr. *Christian Identity and Theological Education*. Atlanta: Scholars, 1985.

Hughy, J. D. "Church, State, and Religious Liberty in Spain." *Journal of Church and State* 23.3 (Autumn 1981) 485–95. https://www.jstor.org/stable/23916758.

Instituto Nacional de Estadística. "Cifras de Población (CP) a 1 de julio de 2022: Estadística de Migraciones (EM); Primer semestre de 2022." Nov. 18, 2022. https://www.ine.es/prensa/cp_j2022_p.pdf.

Istileulova, Yelena, and Darja Peljhan. "Institutional Change as a Result of International Accreditation: Business Schools of Lithuania after the Iron Curtain." *Economic and Business Review* 17.3 (2015) 291–312. https://doi.org/10.15458/85451.8.

Izquierdo, Mario, et al. "Spain: From Massive Immigration to Vast Emigration?" *IZA Journal of Migration* 5.10 (2016). https://doi.org/10.1186/s40176-016-0058-y.

Jackson, Walter C. "A Brief History of Theological Education Including a Description of the Contribution of Wayne E Oates." *Review & Expositor* 94.4 (1997) 503–20. https://doi.org/10.1177/003463739709400403.

Joseph, Celucien L. *Theological Education and Christian Scholarship for Human Flourishing: Hermeneutics, Knowledge, and Multiculturalism*. Eugene, OR: Pickwick, 2022. Kindle.

Kelsey, David H. *Between Athens and Berlin: The Theological Education Debate*. Eugene, OR: Wipf & Stock, 2011.

———. *To Understand God Truly: What's Theological about a Theological School*. Louisville: Westminster John Knox, 1992.

Kelsey, Morton T. *Caring: How Can We Love One Another*. Ramsey, NJ: Paulist, 1981.

Krueger, Richard A., and Mary Anne Casey. *Focus Groups: A Practical Guide for Applied Research*. 3rd ed. Thousand Oaks, CA: SAGE, 2000.

Le Cornu, Alison. "The Shape of Things to Come: Theological Education in the 21st Century." *British Journal of Theological Education* 14.1 (2003) 13–26. https://doi.org/doi:10.1558/jate.v14i1.13.

Luttikhuizen, Frances. *Underground Protestantism in Sixteenth Century Spain: A Much Ignored Side of Spanish History*. Refo500 Academic Studies 30. Gottingen: Vandenhoeck & Ruprecht, 2017.

Ma, Wonsuk. "The Role of Theological Education in Global Mission." Lausanne Consultation on Global Theological Education, May 29–June 1, 2012. YouTube, 16:50. Gordon-Conwell Theological Seminary. https://lausanne.org/video/the-role-of-theological-education-in-global-mission-4.

Macklin, John. "Religion and Modernity in Spain: Religious Experience in the Novels or Ramon Perez de Ayala." *Bulletin of Spanish Studies* 88.7–8 (2011) 183–99. https://doi.org/10.1080/14753820.2011.620316.

Maddox, Randy L. "John Wesley: Practical Theologian?" *Wesleyan Theological Journal* 23.1 (Spring–Fall 1988) 122–47. https://divinity.duke.edu/sites/default/files/documents/07_John_Wesley-Practical_Theologian.pdf.

Martín Díaz, Emma, et al. "Latin American Immigration to Spain: Discourses and Practices from 'La Madre Patria.'" *Cultural Studies* 26.6 (Nov. 2012) 814–41. https://doi.org/10.1080/09502386.2012.669774.

McCulloch, David. "Developing an 'Oslo Model' of Theological Education by Distance Learning for the Contemporary British Church of the Nazarene." PhD diss., University of Glasgow, 2001. http://theses.gla.ac.uk/2108/.

McGrath, Alistair. "What Is Theological Education?" Theological Education Forum, Dec. 9, 2011. http://theologicaleducation.net/articles/view.htm?id=76.

Miller, Sharon L., et al. "Making Connections: A Guide for Conducting Perception Studies." Edited by David Bushko. Auburn Resources. New York: Auburn Theological Seminary, 2002. https://auburnseminary.org/wp-content/uploads/2016/05/Making-Connections_0.pdf.

Montañés, Antonio. "Interacciones entre cultura(s) y religión en minorías socio-religiosas: El caso de los musulmanes y evangélicos-pentecostales en España." *Papeles del CEIC* 3.142 (2015) 1–28. http://dx.doi.org/10.1387/pceic.14604.

Morgan, Donn. "As through a Glass Darkly: Defining Theological Education in the 21st Century." *Anglican Theological Review* 90.2 (2008) 255–65. http://www.anglicantheologicalreview.org/wp-content/uploads/2020/01/morgan_90.2.pdf.

Moschella, Mary Clark. *Ethnography as a Pastoral Practice: An Introduction.* Cleveland, OH: Pilgrim, 2008.

Mwangi, James K., and Ben J. de Klerk. "An Integrated Competency-Based Training Model for Theological Training." *HTS Theological Studies* 67.2 (2011) 1–10. https://doi.org/10.4102/hts.v67i2.1036.

Niebuhr, H. Richard. *The Purpose of the Church and Its Ministry: Reflections on the Aims of Theological Education.* New York: Harper & Brothers, 1956.

"Nuestras comunidades en España." *Cristianismo anabautista.* https://www.menonitas.org/iglesias.html.

Osmer, Richard R. *Practical Theology: An Introduction.* Grand Rapids: Eerdmans, 2008.

Ott, Bernhard. *Beyond Fragmentation: Integrating Mission and Theological Education: A Critical Assessment of Some Recent Developments in Evangelical Theological Education.* Regnum Studies in Mission. Eugene, OR: Wipf & Stock, 2001.

———. "Mission and Theological Education." *Transformation* 18.2 (2001) 87–98. http://www.jstor.org/stable/43053932.

———. *Understanding and Developing Theological Education.* ICETE Series. Carlisle, UK: Langham Global Library, 2016.

Oxenham, Marvin. *Higher Education in Liquid Modernity.* Routledge International Studies in the Philosophy of Education. New York: Routledge, 2013. Kindle.

Payne, Stanley G. *The Collapse of the Spanish Republic, 1933-1936: Origins of the Civil War.* New Haven: Yale University Press, 2006. https://www.jstor.org/stable/j.ctt1npmsx.4.

Pitkanen, Pekka. "Hermits, Closed Orders and Congregations: Issues around Promoting Communities of Theological Scholarship in a Globalized and IT-Brokered World." *Discourse* 9.2 (Spring 2010) 149–64.

Porto, Melina, and Leticia Yulita. "Is There a Place for Forgiveness and Discomforting Pedagogies in the Foreign Language Classroom in Higher Education?" *Cambridge Journal of Education* 49.4 (2019) 477–99. https://doi.org/10.1080/0305764X.2019.1566441.

"Programa de formación teológica a distancia." UEBE Facultad de Teología. https://ftuebe.es/programa-de-formacion-teologica-a-distancia/.

"Quienes somos." CTK, last modified Dec. 3, 2013. https://www.ceteka.org/mod/page/view.php?id=3.

"Quienes somos." Fundación Federico Fliedner. https://www.fliedner.es/es/quienes-somos?lang=es&quienes-somos-fundacion-federico-fliedner.

"Reside con nosotros en la facultad." UEBE Facultad de Teología. https://ftuebe.es/residencia/.

Rooy, Sidney. "Historical Models of Theological Education." In *New Alternatives in Theological Education*, edited by C. René Padilla, 51–72. Oxford: Regnum, 1988.

Roscoe, J. E. *A Short History of Theological Education*. London: Mitre, 1948.

Rosell, Sergio, et al. "CTK: Aprender en comunidad." *Protestante Digital*, Apr. 25, 2014. https://www.protestantedigital.com/muy-personal/14413/ctk-aprender-en-comunidad.

Rowdon, Harold H. "Theological Education in Historical Perspective." *Vox Evangélica* 7 (1971) 75–87. https://biblicalstudies.org.uk/pdf/vox/vol07/education_rowdon.pdf.

S41 Auditoría y Consultoría. "Informe de auditoría de cuentas agregadas emitidos por un auditor independiente: Al patronato de Fundación Federico Fliedner." Madrid, Feb. 14, 2020. https://www.fliedner.es/media/modules/news/182/informe-auditoria-y-cuentas-agregadas-18-19.pdf.

———. "Informe de auditoría de cuentas agregadas emitidos por un auditor independiente: Al patronato de Fundación Federico Fliedner." Madrid, Feb. 8, 2024. chrome-extension://efaidnbmnnnibpcajpcglclefindmkaj/https://www.fliedner.es//media/modules/news/182/ccaa-2022-fff-definitiva---informe-auditoria.pdf.

Sánchez, José Pablo. "El Drama de la España no alcanzada según el ultimo padrón." *Decisión*, June 4, 2019. https://decision.plus/el-drama-de-la-espana-no-alcanzada-segun-el-ultimo-padron/.

Saracco, J. Norberto. "La búsqueda de nuevos modelos de educación teológica." In *Nuevas alternativas de educación teológica*, edited by C. René Padilla, 23–31. Buenos Aires: Nueva Creación; Grand Rapids: Eerdmans, 1986.

Schleiermacher, Friedrich. *Brief Outline of the Study of Theology: Drawn Up to Serve as the Basis of Introductory Lectures* (1850). Translated by William Farrer. Eugene, OR: Wipf & Stock, 2007.

"Se constituye formalmente la Comisión para Acreditación de Centros y Títulos de Teología Protestante." *Actualidad Evangélica*, Nov. 9, 2011. https://www.actualidadevangelica.es/index.php?option=com_content&view=article&id=3345:se-constituye-formalmente-la-comision-para-acreditacion-de-centros-y-titulos-de-teologia-Protestante&catid=46:actualidad.

Seoane, Susana Sueiro. "Spain during the Transition from Dictatorship to Democracy." *Contemporary European History* 13.3 (Aug. 2004) 367–74. https://doi.org/10.1017/S096077730400178X.

Shaw, Perry. *Transforming Theological Education: A Practical Handbook for Integrative Learning*. Carlisle, UK: Langham Global Library, 2014.

Spach, Robert C. "Juan Gil and Sixteenth Century Protestantism." *The Sixteenth Century Journal* 26.4 (Winter 1995) 857–79. https://www.jstor.org/stable/2543791.

Sun, Chloe T. *Attempt Great Things for God: Theological Education in Disapora*. Theological Education Between the Times. Grand Rapids: Eerdmans, 2020. Kindle.

SEUT Facultad de Teología. "Informe de la facultad de teologia SEUT al LXXIX sínodo de la IEE: Cursos 2019–2020 y 2020–2021." https://www.fliedner.es//media/modules/editor/seut/docs/2022_2023/informe-seut-sinodo-2021.pdf.

———. "Memoria del título de grado en teología." Madrid, May 2019. https://www.fliedner.es//media/modules/editor/seut/docs/memoria-verificada-aneca-facultad-seut-2019.pdf.

———. "Trabajo fin de bachillerato: Guía docente de la asignatura." https://www.fliedner.es/media/modules/editor/seut/docs/guias_docentes/2016_2017/m4201-tra_guiadocentetfb_2018.pdf.

Swinton, John, and Harriet Mowat. *Practical Theology and Quantitative Research*. 2nd ed. London: SCM, 2016.

Tierny-Tello, Mary Beth. "Remembering Childhood: Critical Memory through Text and Image in Miguel Gutiérrez's 'La destrucción del reino.'" *Mosaic* 41.2 (2008) 1–28. http://www.jstor.org/stable/44029493.

"Titulación." Centro Teológica Koinonia, last modified Apr. 15, 2023. https://www.ceteka.org/mod/page/view.php?id=4.

"La titulación de los centros de formación teológica protestantes es reconocida con efectos civiles por el Gobierno de España." *Lupa Protestante*, Nov. 12, 2011. http://www.lupaProtestante.com/blog/la-titulacion-de-los-centros-de-formacion-teologica-Protestantes-son-reconocidas-con-efectos-civiles-por-el-gobierno-de-espana/.

Tortell, Philippe, et al. "Remembering Is Crucial to Our Future." *The Tyee*, Nov. 8, 2019. https://thetyee.ca/Opinion/2019/11/08/Remembering-Crucial-To-Our-Future/.

Tromp, Paul, et al. "'Believing without Belonging' in Twenty European Countries (1981–2008) De-institutionalization of Christianity or Spiritualization of Religion?" *Review of Religious Research* 62.4 (2020) 509–31. https://doi.org/10.1007/s13644-020-00432-z.

UEBE Facultad de Teología. "Dossier informativo: Curso académico 2021–2022." Madrid, 2021. https://ftuebe.es/wp-content/uploads/2021/12/Dossier-informativo-2021-22.pdf.

———. "Memoria del título de grado en teología de la facultad de teología UEBE." Madrid, Sept. 20, 2019. https://ftuebe.es/wp-content/uploads/2021/07/mem_grado_ftuebe1.pdf.

Vanhoozer, Kevin J. "From Bible to Theology." In *Theology, Church, and Ministry: A Handbook for Theological Education*, edited by Dockery, David S., 233–56. Nashville: B&H Academic, 2017. Kindle.

———. "What Is Everyday Theology? How and Why Christians Should Read Culture." In *Everyday Theology: How to Read Cultural Texts and Interpret Trends*, edited by Kevin J. Vanhoozer et al., 15–60. Grand Rapids: Baker Academic, 2007.

Villascusa, Angel. "El nuevo auge de los protestantes reta al Estado aconfesional: 'Hay que avanzar en libertad religiosa.'" *El Diario*, Dec. 24, 2018. https://www.eldiario.es/sociedad/evangelicos-espanoles-catolicismo-verdadera-religiosa_1_1781781.html.

Vincent, Mary. "Ungodly Subjects: Protestants in National-Catholic Spain, 1939–53." *European History Quarterly* 45.1 (Jan. 2015) 108–31. https://doi.org/10.1177/0265691414552782.

Ward, Pete. *Introducing Practical Theology: Mission, Ministry and the Life of the Church*. Grand Rapids: Baker Academic, 2017.

www.ingramcontent.com/pod-product-compliance
Lightning Source LLC
Chambersburg PA
CBHW060609230426
43670CB00011B/2038